TANNA HORTON

audience of one

IN A WORLD WITH MANY *Audiences*, SEEK THE *One* THAT TRULY MATTERS.

Audience of One

61Press LLC
ron@61press.com

ISBN 978-1-965775-03-5

Cover Design & Interior Design by Tessa Schoumaker, 3Pier Creative Agency
Printed in the United States of America

First edition: January 2025

CONTENTS

DEDICATION

To my husband, my children and my people. You were my motivation to do the hard work to become the best version of myself I could be.

Brandon Heath, you have shown me the most beautiful, Christ-like and unconditional love that I could have ever imagined. Thank you, I couldn't have done this without you.

Brylee, Cerly, Audree and Heath; My heart is for you to know Jesus personally and to feel the Holy Spirit working in your life daily. The world you're growing up in will pull you in every direction, so my prayer is for each of you to learn from my mistakes to avoid unnecessary pain in your life.

To my people; You never gave up on me, even when I was hard to love. I could never thank you enough.

NOTE FROM AUTHOR

Audience of One is a vision God gave me years ago when I began to recognize the many ways I was living with a desire to please people over Him. As you read this book, my prayer is that God will open your eyes to the freedom found when you choose Him above all else. As a mom of four, I understand the busyness of life and the distractions that are constantly thrown our way. The book is designed to be read one chapter at a time, similar to a devotional. Take your time as you go through each chapter so you don't miss what God wants to show you. Allow yourself time to process what you've read and work through things the Lord reveals before moving to the next chapter. There may be some chapters or subjects that feel harder to digest, and I encourage you to re-read them if you need to. Learning how to have an audience of one in every area has taken me years, and it's not something that can be conquered overnight. Give yourself time and grace so that God can purify you from the inside out. Enjoy the journey!

the vision: christ be magnified

"In my life or in my death, Christ will be magnified in me."

PHILIPPIANS 1:20

In August of 2021, I was driving on the highway, headed to church to join my friend, Ashley, for a worship service. I will never forget this drive. It was the drive where God gave me a very clear visual of Audience of One. I was about halfway to the church when I saw a room full of hundreds of blindfolded women. He had my attention immediately because He had never shown me anything like that before. Not only were they blindfolded, but every single hand was in the air all over the room. Picture that for a second, hundreds of women all worshiping, all in, completely surrendered to the Lord. The attention in the room was on one thing, our Lord Jesus. There wasn't a single distracted soul worrying about who was around them or who might be watching them. I kept driving as God began to unfold this vision for me. It was the most beautiful picture I had ever seen. As tears fell down my cheeks, I had to pull my car over because I was completely overwhelmed. I couldn't drive because of the weight of the words I heard. Over and over I heard "Audience of One." I sat on the side of the highway for a few minutes, taking it all in, constantly wiping the tears as they fell and soaked my shirt. I had a picture He had shown me and words He had told me, but I wouldn't know what it all meant until nearly two years later.

For a long time, I thought that Audience of One was supposed to be a women's event where many women would come to a church for one evening of worship. It wasn't until June of 2023 when God revealed to me that learning to have an audience of one wouldn't be possible in a two-hour event. Learning to have an audience of one would take time and require constant effort towards growth. It was at that moment when God began to give me the chapter titles. I will never forget it. I was on a plane headed to Belize while I wrote as fast as I could as He revealed every area where He has taught me to seek an audience of one. Within minutes, I had every chapter title in this book. I knew without a doubt that the next step was to start writing the first chapter.

Most of us wake up each day with different audiences depending on the situation. Our entire days are spent seeking the approval of others and living in a way where our eyes are fixated on the wrong things. Our audience is many, which is why we tend to feel exhausted and defeated by the end of the day. When God initially gave me the vision for Audience of One, I wondered why He used blindfolded women who were worshiping to help me understand His heart. Throughout my writing, I have seen the heart of a woman in so many areas. I believe our obedience starts with our worship.

Just recently, I could feel a tug in my heart. It was like I had one more step to take in this. God then revealed to me that my worship was not fully surrendered to Him. I have always been able to worship freely without worrying too much about who was around me, but throughout this journey He told me that there was still a piece of my heart holding back during worship. It was a normal Sunday morning at church when I felt the Holy Spirit nudging me to lift both of my hands as if I was in full surrender. I fought the urge for a moment, thinking that I didn't want to be doing too much or be too into it.

I knew right then that seeking an audience of one must start through my worship because my worship had so many strings attached to it. What was the song? Who was sitting next to me or behind me that day? What church was I at and would it be too much? We can't have strings attached to our worship because if we do then those strings will be attached to every other area of our lives. Choosing to fully surrender on that Sunday morning freed up my heart in a new way. If we can completely abandon our flesh during worship, then our heart is exactly where it needs to be as it leaves church and heads into the real world. I love the old song called "Heart of Worship" because it reminds us that worship is all about Him and not about us. Understanding those words will change everything for us.

Through each chapter, my heart is to express how God has walked me through every area of my life in order to show me that I was living in a way that wasn't pleasing to Him. As you will see, it has been quite the journey, but it was a journey worth choosing to face. I feel like every time I learned how to shift the focus of my audience, I was able to cut a rope that had been choking me for so many years. It's not until you find freedom from something before you fully feel the grip that it had on you. I have been able to cut a lot of ropes over the years, which is why I finally feel healthy from the inside out. I want that for each of you too!

A few years ago, God gave me a new song that has become my theme song for this journey. It is called "Christ be Magnified" by Cody Carnes. I had never heard this song until the worship pastor sang it one Sunday morning. Since then, I have played it over and over. Laundry is a big chore in my house since we have four kids. I made a vow that I would play this song every time I folded laundry and let God teach me through it. You can imagine how many times I have heard it over the last two years.

To magnify means to honor something. If there is one thing I hope you will remember after reading this book it is this. The only way we can honor God through each part of our life is to seek His audience and His audience alone. When our audience is others, then our motives are usually impure. When our audience is our kids, then our actions are typically unhealthy and not what is best for our children. When our audience is focused on performing or achieving success, then our heart is usually swirling in selfishness or pride. When our audience is fear, whether it's during worship or anything else, then we are often operating in disobedience. The only time we walk in complete purity is when we choose to be obedient regardless of the cost or sacrifice. Ultimately, the reason we are here on Earth is so that Christ can be magnified through our lives.

Seek His audience and His audience alone.

chapter one:
a second chance

"For we know that all things work together for the good of those who love him, who have been called according to His purpose."

ROMANS 8:28

I can't remember a day when I didn't know Jesus. I was born into a home that taught me about Jesus from the moment I could understand, so He has always been present in my life and in my heart. While growing up, despite the ups and downs that came my way, He was someone I prayed to, someone I found security in, and someone who was a constant in my life. I had a sweet knowledge of Him and would often feel the Holy Spirit in my heart, which brought me a special comfort that nothing else could.

As I moved into high school, Jesus was the one who kept me grounded. He was my accountability when no one was watching. Somehow I managed to make it through those years without many regrets. My core friend group shared my same beliefs, so it was easier to choose right over wrong regardless of the temptations.

My first year of college was a bit different. My friend circle changed, I was out on my own, and I started acting completely out of character. The pull to fit in with my sorority was strong, and I found myself in compromising situations. Even then, I was thankful because I had the Holy Spirit on the other side of the seesaw. Every time I tried to do things my way, I would have the Holy Spirit pressuring down on the other side to bring me back to reality. Luckily, my parents helped me transfer to a new college where I grew in my faith and was surrounded by others wanting to do the same thing. The decision to transfer after freshman year was life-changing in the best way, which I will forever be thankful for.

I wish I could say that things have been smooth sailing since my college graduation, but if I am being honest, I don't think that I fully knew the heart of Jesus until I was 36 years old. It's easy to say you trust Him when that is all you have ever known. It's easy to believe He can do all things when you haven't faced something that seemed impossible for your human eyes. However, once you have come face-to-face with pain, suffering, sin, deep depression, unimaginable regret, and complete loss, that is when Jesus gets to show you who He really is.

It is in those difficult moments where Jesus gets to shine and show up for you in a way that you don't deserve or can even comprehend.

Today, I can look in the mirror and say that Jesus is my rescuer. Yes, I believe I was saved as a five-year-old little girl, but I didn't surrender my life to Him until I was a 36-year-old wife and mom. After I crumbled and recognized my deep need for Him, he began to turn the impossible into something beautiful. He took my brokenness and has slowly unveiled what it looks like to build my foundation and my family on Him alone.

My family is my world and they are the reason I am here writing this today. I bring them up in the following chapters, so I want to give a little insight into who they are. My husband, Brandon, is my very best friend. I can't remember life without him. The two of us met at church when we were 12 years old, so he has always been a constant in my life. We were friends for many years, long before we realized we shared a deeper love for one another. Brandon is faithful, he is thoughtful, and his heart is filled with unconditional love.

We have four children, three girls and one boy. Our 16-year-old, Brylee, is the one who taught me how to be a mom. When she was younger, I remember telling her that I was learning with her and that I would need grace over the years. Not only has Brylee given me grace, but she brings stability to our home, she is a wonderful role model for her siblings, and her heart for others is so pure. Brylee has a unique sensitivity about her that shows up in moments where others need it most. I always say how Brylee is a beautiful blend of Brandon and me. She is logical, she is compassionate, and her thoughtfulness amazes me. Not only does she challenge me to be my best each day, but her life changed me from the day she was born.

Our 14-year-old, Cerly, brings accountability to my life in a way that only she can do. Ever since Cerly was little, her heart felt conviction differently than my other girls. Her sensitivity to things that are not of God is very present and that encourages all of us to do better. Cerly is loyal, she is consistent, and she sees people when others don't. We used to wonder if she ever listened or knew what was going on around her. As she got older, we realized that she is always aware of her surroundings; however, she is not quick to be expressive with her thoughts. Therefore, I am completely tuned in when she does express her heart because I know it will be special.

Our 12-year-old, Audree, is my mini-me who brings so much fun to our lives. I can't remember a time when Audree wasn't dancing, performing, or being who God created her to be. What I love most about Audree is the confidence she walks in, never worrying about what others think. Audree has first-born tendencies, along with a carefree spirit for life. When I think of Audree, I also think of her affection. Audree sees me in the midst of the chaos and is always close by for a hug when I need it most. There are times she will try to tiptoe the line with her words, but it doesn't take long before her heart wants to pray and do better. Audree is bold in every way, and I feel God will use that boldness to help her lead well.

Heath Robert is our nine-year-old little boy who completed our family in a way we could have never dreamed of. God knew we needed him long before we knew. Heath came into my life when my heart was hurting, and God used him to teach me the beauty of restoration. Heath is named after Brandon, my Papa, and my dad. I tell you this because Heath is a perfect mix of these special men in my life. I constantly see their characteristics reflected in him. Heath is not only thoughtful in his actions, but he has the ability to see a need before you even have a chance to ask for help. He is athletic, his spirit is sensitive, and his smile can make anything better.

I always imagined my life would be filled with pretty rainbows, and even though the rainbows are there, I will tell you they didn't come without the true testing of my faith. Parts of my story will unfold slowly throughout each chapter, and I pray that God will use each piece to bring breakthroughs and growth into your life. God continually reminds me each day that one choice, good or bad, can completely change the direction of my life. For that reason, I must stay grounded without wavering. He has taught me the importance of keeping my thoughts and my actions in the light because the Enemy only works in the dark. Once I fully understood my need for grace, I was able to fully understand His ability to give grace. To me, God is the god of second chances and fresh starts. He redeemed my heart, my family, and my future. For that, He is everything to me.

PROCESS AND REFLECT:

- Before we go any further, I want to ask you a question. Does Jesus live in your heart in such a way where you feel His spirit constantly guiding you? If you aren't sure, come talk to me or someone you know about this. Until we understand what it means to accept Jesus into our heart, and live in the Spirit, it's very difficult to learn how to seek an audience of one.

chapter two: fully known

"Search me, oh God, and know my heart; test me and know my anxious thoughts. See if there is anything offensive in me, and lead me in the way everlasting."

PSALM 139:23-24

I felt seen for the first time in my 7th grade home economics class. I suppose I had felt seen by my family growing up—to a certain extent—but this was different. This is the first memory I have of someone seeing me and using it to hurt me. I was 12 years old and a boy sitting at my table made fun of my teeth. I can still see his face as he laughed at me and told me that I had "butter teeth." For some reason, this hit my heart so hard. To this day, I believe it is the root of why I began to seek the approval of others for so many years.

When God gave me the vision to write this book, I asked Him where it all started for me. Where did my insecurities begin? I asked Him to show me why I struggled for so long caring about what others thought of me and making sure they were always happy with me. It didn't take long before He showed me the 12-year-old girl sitting at that table being so wounded by the words of another person. The truth is that even the smallest hurts or painful words can become so deeply rooted in us that it alters our behaviors long term. Whether we want to admit it or not, unhealthy behaviors flow through all of us because of the baggage we carry. We can either choose to swim in it or we can swim away from it. I will be honest, both options are hard because pain is hard, but we will only find true freedom when we choose to swim away from it by allowing God to heal each piece. Learning to have an audience of one in Christ is not a one-time decision; it's a journey that we must go on and walk through daily.

My girls are entering into the preteen and teenage years, which has really turned up the pressure for me. I have always had six little girl eyes on me. Every one of my actions and reactions is witnessed by them, which is a huge responsibility. I remember them watching me put on my makeup in the mirror when they were little. They would mimic me and it was the sweetest thing. They watched as I picked up the blush, then they would pick it up too and put it on.

Things changed inside of me when God revealed to me that my daughters were my "why."

During a sermon, I heard something that has really stuck with me: "If we know our why, then we can get through any how." At the time, I had been swimming in the unhealth of caring what others thought of me for over 25 years. I realized that I was living with the wrong audience! I was living for an audience of others, fearing that someone might not approve of me, which is why I was never able to escape the unhealthy mindset. I needed a new audience. If my three girls were watching me do something as trivial as putting on makeup, then they were definitely watching all of the ways I was operating in my life. The day my girls became my why was the day I chose to start swimming away from the unhealthy mindset. Sometimes doing hard things for ourselves seems impossible, but choosing to do it for my daughters started a fire in me that still passionately burns within me.

What God has shown me is that we don't know how to be fully seen, all the baggage included, and feel fully loved at the same time.

This journey starts with recognizing that all of us find ourselves seeking the wrong audiences for many different reasons. We all carry baggage with different labels due to the unique upbringings and past experiences that we have walked through. In that regard, we are different, but it didn't take long for God to begin to show me how we are all the same. Even though our pain is unique to us, we all want to be seen and loved. I have never met a woman who didn't share in these desires. There are some that don't want to be seen on a stage. They might prefer being seen and appreciated by their spouse in their home or by a close friend. It's ironic though because we do desire for others to see our hearts, but many of us spend endless hours creating posts and reels on Instagram that tell a different story.

What God has shown me is that we don't know how to be fully seen, all the baggage included, and feel fully loved at the same time. Because of that, we live lives that can seem shallow, fake, or even appear perfect in an attempt to hide the insecurities in our hearts. I have spent years trying to understand how to be fully known by others without fighting the fears that shame and baggage weigh my thoughts down with. The truth is, I don't think it's possible to do it until you choose to be fully known by God and fully believe that He loves you despite your mistakes.

I was watching an episode of The Chosen when God revealed His love to me in a way that changed me. Mary Magdalene had spent years fighting demonic episodes. She had tried all sorts of remedies to seek freedom from this, but she was left with the same mental battle each time until Jesus touched her and healed her. It was later in the show when she met eyes with Jesus again, and I literally felt like her when I saw her face. She knew at that moment that Jesus saw her. She felt fully seen for the first time in her life. He knew her past and still pursued her. I believe He pursued her because He also saw her beauty, He saw her heart, and He saw redemption. Her smile of joy was a beautiful picture of what it means to understand that we are fully known and fully loved by God at the same time.

When God restores us, he purifies us with a fresh start. The world and the audience of others is not capable of offering us this gift, which is why we will never find freedom through seeking the approval of others. Not only will we not find freedom, but we will dig the deepest and most suffocating prison by choosing to live this way. So, why do so many of us do it? For me, it was fear of rejection and acceptance, but honestly I just didn't know how to do it any other way. Old habits are hard to break, and sometimes unhealthy is comfortable to us because we know what to expect even though it is miserable. Learning to have an audience of one is not a one-time decision. This book is my personal journey of how God took me through every moment of my life and taught me how to choose more wisely. This journey was by far

When God restores us, he purifies us with a fresh start.

the hardest thing I have ever had to walk through, but the testimony He gave me through the journey is priceless.

Brandon and my children are my "why" because as the mom of this home, it's important that I learn to seek an audience of one in every area of my life. I can wake up each day and provide them with everything that I think they need, but if I don't get this right then they too might leave my home without knowing who their audience should be. They are growing up in a very loud and dark world where the audiences are many. I need God to use me to leave a mark on their hearts that they will carry with them. Moms, it starts with us!

I promise you it is possible to be fully known and fully loved at the same time. I can't wait for you to go on this journey with me!

If we were all honest, we could probably identify the moment where someone saw us in a negative light for the first time. Maybe you're like me and it was a classmate who chose to humiliate or make fun of you. It's time to get honest with ourselves, to dig deep, and to dive into this journey. Through each chapter, I write about how God showed me all the layers to having an audience of one and how I truly walked in the Spirit in order to experience it. I promise you it is possible to be fully known and fully loved at the same time. I can't wait for you to go on this journey with me!

PROCESS AND REFLECT:

- Can you think of a time when you felt seen in a negative light? Do you think you have insecurities that stem from this?
- What are some areas in your life you are scared for others to see? Why do you feel scared to be fully known in this area?

3

chapter three: complete brokenness

"For everyone that exalts himself will be humbled, and he who humbles himself will be exalted."

LUKE 14:11

As I sit down to write this chapter today, I am feeling every single emotion. In order to go back to the place where God had to get my attention, I knew I would have to revisit a very difficult time in my life. You may be reading this today with different struggles than mine. If you're open to it, I can assure you that this part of my story will connect with you on some level. It's the part of my story where I found myself battling with pride, control, depression, sin, immeasurable pain, and complete loss and was in desperate need of hope.

It's the part of my story where I found myself battling with pride, control, depression, sin, immeasurable pain, and complete loss and was in desperate need of hope.

At one time, I had served in women's ministry at our church for about six years. I will share more detail on this later, but my heart has always had a special place for women and a strong desire to help them. Throughout my years of ministry, I would often feel the Holy Spirit burdening my heart to speak on certain topics or lead the women in certain ways. When I began serving I was very obedient to the Lord, but over time I started to allow the fear of man to seep in. After about three years, I was officially added to the church staff and began planning events with a people-pleasing mentality and pushed aside things I knew God had asked me to do or share. It didn't take long before my audience became women. My heart wasn't faithful to what God had called me to do. As the complaints from the women built up, I realized I couldn't make them all happy. I began to change the way I thought and operated in ministry. Looking back, I would have called this "the slow fade" because it was the beginning of the end for me.

During that time, the unhealthiness in me was camouflaged because I was being praised for doing so many good things when it came to counseling women and spending every second

I had to help in any way I could. My heart was all in, but I was starting to operate on my own strength, telling myself that I could do it all on my own. I remember being told that I was a high-functioning staff member. This fueled the pride in me, causing me to take on more and more in an attempt to be seen as worthy and good enough. It is hard to pinpoint the exact moment I realized that I was in trouble and that my family was suffering, but in my last year on staff I found myself saving everyone else's family while slowly losing mine. I didn't mean for this to happen, but I was giving all of my energy to the women who were trying to save their marriages and their homes. I was using all of my emotional love tank for others while sacrificing my own home.

There is a reason Scripture tells us to be alert and to put on the full armor of God each day. I took my eyes off the Lord and put my focus on people, which led me down a dark path. The slow fade of losing my focus gained momentum and the Enemy invaded my thoughts, my home, and my life in the worst ways. Brandon and I had been married for about 11 years and our marriage was nowhere close to where it needed to be. Christ was not the center of our marriage and I had nothing left to give by the end of the night. I went from helping women to literally laying on my face crying every time a woman complained about an event or something that I had tried my best to make wonderful. I was consuming any and every kind of sleeping medication in an attempt to rest because my mind would never stop racing. To make the circus in my mind stop, I used anything I could get my hands on (bottles of Benadryl, pain meds, muscle relaxers). I was on anxiety medication, my boundaries were blurry in all areas, and I had random drinking outings to try and escape all I was feeling. I had so many people around me, yet I felt so alone. I continued to show up on Sunday mornings with a smile on my face even though I was a complete mess inside. I realized that ministry was a very lonely place if you're not constantly pursuing health along the way.

This was when pride was the most evident in my heart. I was a disaster inside, but I managed to keep the show going for the rest of the world. I was juggling way too much, and it was only a matter of time before I would break. You would have thought I would have been fully aware I had a problem—or many, to say the least—but sometimes when a person is so wrapped up in themselves they fail to see the truth even if it is staring them in the face. I had become so good at hiding my pain that I didn't even have the accountability of my friends because I was fooling them as well. While some of them had started to notice my unusual behavior, I continued to reassure them I was fine even though I was completely crumbling inside. It would take a whole second book to write about all the experiences that followed, but just know I wouldn't wish them on anyone. Some things were in my control while others were completely out of my control, but the destruction was brutal. My children were attacked, my marriage was attacked, my friendships were attacked, the women's ministry was attacked, and I couldn't stand it anymore.

One night, I found myself hiding in my closet. My closet had become my go-to place for when I was hurting and I was in there quite often. On this night, I was feeling more broken than I had ever felt. I had just put my four babies to bed and the Enemy was screaming that I would never be good enough for anything, not even to be their mom. Being a mom was one of my biggest joys and my love for them was so deep, but that night I felt like such a failure in this area. I am not sure if you have ever experienced spiritual warfare or not, but I promise you it's a real thing. That night, I believe that darkness was fighting for my life and it almost won.

I decided that I didn't want to live another day. My thoughts were telling me that my children and my husband would be better off without me. I couldn't breathe because my chest was so heavy. My pillow was covered in black from all the mascara I had worn that day to hide the pain. I sat in that closet, took sleeping medication, and hoped that I would never wake up. I wholeheartedly believed I wasn't strong enough to overcome the darkness, but God used my sister's obedience to shine the light I needed in that exact moment. I heard a ding on my phone. That ding broke the darkness that had been filling up my closet. Audra was texting, just to check in on me and tell me that she loved and needed me. There was nothing unique about her words that night. Her words didn't change anything or fix me, but God used her words as a weapon to help battle the Enemy I was facing at that moment. The darkness began to break when I read that my sister needed me. Even if I didn't believe it at the time, my family wasn't better off without me. They needed me too.

A big step towards humility is asking God or others that love you to shine a light on your life so that the pride is in the open and can be dealt with.

The journey of healing that followed that night was years long and extremely difficult, but it was important that I share this early on in the book because learning to have an audience of one is so much about recognizing that we can't do anything without Christ. Sure, we can do it for a while; I was living proof of that. However, there will always come a time when we will break. It may take tragedy, traumatic events, loss, an unfortunate diagnosis, or something happening with our children, but we will all face moments where we will break if our audience is not Him and Him alone. Walking through that time, I also realized that a person can have everything in front of them to live for and still feel like they can't get through one more day. I had five people who loved me deeply and a wonderful life in front of me, but depression doesn't discriminate. The darkness was more real than I could have ever imagined, and I am forever thankful for my sister's obedience to text me that night. If you find yourself in that place today, I want you to know that I see you and I promise you that there is hope.

Humility is a heartbreaking lesson, but God desires for us to walk through this life with a humbled heart. A big step towards humility is asking God or others that love you to shine a light on your life so that the pride is in the open and can be dealt with. It was hard for me to see it in myself, but when I allowed others to have a voice in my life they were able to help identify the areas in need of attention.

Being stripped of pride or any other sin is painful but absolutely necessary if we want to live a life with our eyes fixed on Jesus.

After that dark night, I didn't have one ounce of pride left because I had almost lost everything, including my life. Complete brokenness is what it took in order for God to show me my need for a savior. I had known Jesus since I was a little girl, but it was that night where I found my Savior. All of our hearts are filled with pride, which shows up differently for each one of us. The Bible is very clear when it says that we are to humble ourselves or we will be humbled. Being stripped of pride or any other sin is painful but absolutely necessary if we want to live a life with our eyes fixed on Jesus. The bible says the children of God will be disciplined, and for me, this was a very significant way in which God disciplined me. For many years I viewed God's discipline as harsh, almost like a negative thing. It wasn't until I saw the heart of God through His discipline was I able to grasp my need for this in my life. In Hebrews 12: 5-6, it says not to underestimate the value of discipline and training from the Lord, and then goes on to say we should welcome this in our life. So many times the things we stiff arm are the very things we need to be embracing. For me, the road to humility purified me even though it was the hardest road I have ever had to walk.

PROCESS AND REFLECT:

- How do you struggle with pride in your life?
- Do you think it's obvious to others or are you masking it like I was?

chapter four: baby steps

"Trust in the Lord with all your heart and lean not on your own understanding. Acknowledge Him in all your ways and He will make your path straight."

PROVERBS 3:5-6

At 22, Brandon proposed to me using glow-in-the-dark baby feet to create a pathway for me to follow that led me to him. I remember my heart was racing that night the moment I realized what was coming. Every time I stepped forward, I knew I was one step closer to him. With each step, my heart filled with excitement. I knew once I finally made it to him then all of my dreams would come true.

Over the years, "baby steps" has become a thing for us. Whether it's been related to our marriage or trying to navigate how to raise our children, we often remind each other to take baby steps. One step at a time seems easier than trying to figure everything out at once. I've learned that taking one step at a time also allows for processing time, which usually leads to growth.

I told you earlier that my road to healing was very long. It was filled with many, many baby steps. After that life-altering night I was encouraged to take one big step in obedience. I was made aware of an intense, long weekend away known as Fully Alive. I had already declined the offer to go because I was convinced I didn't have time for it. I had no idea what I would do with my four little ones for that long, and I honestly didn't think it would help me. It seemed like a lot of work just to get there, so I decided it wasn't for me. Shortly after the dark night, when everything felt like it was crumbling, I was asked again to consider making it a priority to attend Fully Alive. I can't remember what exactly led me to say yes, but I finally agreed and packed my bags. At this point, no one knew the depth of my pain nor did they know about the deep depression. I had continued to hang on to that secret night as if it was sacred, or maybe it was my pride not wanting anyone to know what a failure I felt like. Regardless, when I arrived I walked into a house with about 20 other women and had no idea what would go down in the days to follow.

I love the passage in the Bible where Jesus approaches the man who had been crippled since

If you truly want to change, you have to be willing to do whatever it takes regardless of how difficult it is.

he was a young boy. Jesus asks him, "Do you want to be healed?" It's a great question. It's like when a person says they want to lose weight and get healthy but they are unwilling to change their diet. They really don't want to lose weight that badly or else they would be willing to make the sacrifice. If you truly want to change, you have to be willing to do whatever it takes regardless of how difficult it is. I think many of us think we want to get better, but we are unwilling to take the steps in order to make it happen.

I understand this is hard to hear because it was for me, but part of growth is being able to hear hard things without a defensive heart.

Every kind of healing or change doesn't happen on its own. I believe that many would rather stay sick than do the hard work. I understand this is hard to hear because it was for me, but part of growth is being able to hear hard things without a defensive heart. A person with a defensive heart typically doesn't want to grow, and they are usually more concerned with how they were offended when they heard the truth. So, step one is asking yourself if you're ready to consistently do the work to get to the other side regardless of what mountain is in front of you. Finding freedom from any type of bondage is a fight, whether it's an addiction, a mental health issue, a past hurt, or learning what it looks like to truly forgive. You have to be ready for the fight and be willing to do whatever it takes. Sometimes it takes a huge step of obedience in order to find the strength to take 50 more small steps towards healing. This weekend retreat was my big step and that step was me screaming loudly, "I am ready to be healed no matter the cost!"

I remember the first session where they made us all sit in a circle to share. Yes, I had chosen to go, but I had not yet opened up my heart towards being vulnerable. My friend Shannon and I had a terrible attitude as we sat there judging the whole situation. I had led many types of circle groups before, so I assumed I knew what was coming and refused to take the bait. I spent the first 24 hours with my arms crossed because I wasn't planning to allow anyone in that room to have access to my emotions. I held on strongly for as long as I could, but once the Holy Spirit hit the room I couldn't fight it anymore. The tears began to fall. I tend to hold onto emotional things very tightly, all while keeping my composure, but the Holy Spirit is the one thing I can't fight. It's like I can go up against anyone or anything else, but the power of the Holy Spirit is so heavy that I don't stand a chance. Praise God for that! Once the tears started to fall, they didn't stop for days. It was like everything in me was exposed, and I felt like I could breathe again for the first time in a long time.

My Fully Alive experience was the closest I had ever felt to Jesus. I was a complete mess and felt like my world had crumbled, but I felt His love and acceptance in a beautiful way. We were asked not to share the details of the experience so that we wouldn't ruin it for others, but those moments are forever etched in my soul. Throughout those days, I learned what it meant to starve my flesh, literally, so that my spirit would be strengthened. I experienced authentic vulnerability in front of others, which was huge because as a staff member I never felt I had permission to do so. For once, I showed my humanness and wasn't ashamed. I took steps of obedience that forced me to not care what others thought of me. For so long, I felt like my life was a glass house, all eyes on me, just waiting for me to fail as a leader. That day, I sat in the middle of the carpet floor with all eyes on me, but no one was really looking at me. Not only did they not care about my failures, but they were praying over me, fighting for my family, and speaking the truth to every lie that my head had been screaming for years. For once in my life, my audience was God himself and not anyone or anything else in the world. Countless hours of spiritual victory took place on that carpet over the course of a few days. There is no doubt in my mind that Jesus met me face-to-face on that carpet and proved to me that He was bigger than any darkness that was swirling over my life.

Working through hard things is an accumulation of baby steps, so many baby steps. As I walked away from Fully Alive, it was only the beginning of the healing journey for me. I spent countless hours in Christian counseling, where we worked hard to help me to understand how I ended up in the hole I was in. I began to set necessary boundaries in my life, which allowed me to be surrounded by safe people who I knew had my family's best interest at heart. I sought forgiveness from people I had wounded and began taking steps to rebuild broken trust. Self reflection was vital during this time and I knew I had to look in the mirror in order for God to heal all of the broken pieces. You see, true restoration usually doesn't happen in a moment or at a weekend retreat. For me, the weekend retreat was the place where God got my attention, but it was through each baby step where He slowly healed and put my heart back together.

Saying yes to Fully Alive was me fully surrendering to God even though nothing inside of me believed it would work. Sometimes, all we need is the courage to say yes and the rest will follow. I encourage you to think about your own life and the areas of your heart that need healing and ask Him what step one is. Remember, just focus on one step at a time. Some steps will be fast, while other steps may take weeks or months. In the end, every step matters and will be worth giving it your all.

PROCESS AND REFLECT:

- Is there a big step in your life that you have felt God asking you to take? Or maybe it's a smaller step. Any time you feel that nudge inside, you have to ask yourself what God might be trying to guide you to do.

5

chapter five: the gift of forgiveness

"Let all bitterness and wrath and anger and clamor and slander be put away from you, along with all malice. Be kind to one another, tenderhearted, forgiving one another, as God in Christ forgave you."

EPHESIANS 4:31-32

I made a list of the steps I have walked through in order to understand what it means to seek after an audience of one. Forgiveness is by far the most important step. This step involves learning to forgive but also learning how to ask for forgiveness. I've jokingly said that I'm not sure which one is harder, but after thoroughly living through both of them I think I would rather be the one doing the forgiving. Want to know why? It's because that is the one I can control. Unfortunately, we don't get to decide whether another person will offer us forgiveness, but we do get to decide if we give forgiveness.

You see, when you build up bitterness and hold onto unforgiveness, you begin to live in a world where your reality is not accurate.

I never learned how to forgive until I needed to be forgiven. I think God designed it that way because needing forgiveness is the very best teacher. I am ashamed to admit the long list of things that I had held on to for years and years inside of my heart. That list clouded my thinking and filled my thoughts with constant chaos and insecurity. You see, when you build up bitterness and hold onto unforgiveness, you begin to live in a world where your reality is not accurate. You place motives on people that don't belong there, you misplace anger on those you love, and you make assumptions that constantly end in conflict. Your normal becomes so clouded with mistrust that you start to feel like a crazy person. Anyone feel me? You are yelling at someone in your house about making a mess, but what is actually fueling that anger is bitterness and resentment towards someone else.

Most people who walk around angry and unhappy are that way because they never learned how to offer forgiveness. For years, I carried so much anger because I didn't believe it was possible to forgive and move forward. I really didn't. I had never been taught how to forgive in

I never learned how to forgive until I needed to be forgiven.

a way that stuck. I would forgive one week and then the minute that wound was activated in me again, I would be right back to square one. It was like a scab that could never heal. What's interesting is that a scab on your arm seems to get hit over and over before it finally heals. Have you ever had that happen to you? Or like when you bite the inside of your lip. Your lip is so swollen, which makes it easier to bite it again. It makes my stomach hurt thinking about it because I hate the feeling of biting my lip. I really hate the feeling when I bite it in the same spot a second or third time. It is the worst, and I think it hurts even more after multiple bites. My friends, that is unforgiveness. We relive situations in our mind and replay them over and over to the point where we get angrier each time that area of our heart is accessed. The saddest part is that many of us have multiple wounds inside of us from numerous people, which can keep us constantly operating out of the pain of unforgiveness. It is impossible to have healthy relationships with unforgiveness in your heart.

It is impossible to have healthy relationships with unforgiveness in your heart.

At Fully Alive, we had some alone time outside for several hours. We were supposed to pray and ask God what He wanted us to do that afternoon. I sat staring out on the edge of a rock and had no idea what I was supposed to do. All of a sudden, I looked over and saw this huge steep hill that was about 40 yards long. If you have ever run bleachers, that gives you an idea of how steep it was. I stared at this hill while God told me to set my notebook at the bottom of it and run as fast as I could to the top. I found it to be interesting, but I loved to run so that was something I was capable of doing. I made it to the top pretty easily that first time and that is when God revealed to me that I was going to "walk out forgiveness" for as long as it took.

That was the day I learned that forgiveness was not a one-time thing. At the bottom of the hill, I would write down my hurt on my paper and then sprint to the top. As I sprinted with all my might, I would say the hurt out loud in an attempt to give it to God. As I cried, I would walk back to the bottom and prepare my heart to forgive another hurt. If I felt peace inside then I would cross it off my paper and go to the next hurt. There were things on my list where I didn't find peace after one sprint to the top, so I would run up the hill again, yelling it out because I wanted to let it go so badly.

Some things were easier to let go of than others, but after two hours of running every hurt was crossed off my list. I love marking things off a list. It must be my OCD tendencies or something. When I marked things off my list that day, I not only felt accomplished, but I felt free. Free from the chains that had choked me day after day. Free from marriage hurts that I had been carrying for over 13 years. Free from the pain my mother-in-law caused by making me feel like I was never good enough for her son. Free from the comments by women that years of women's ministry had laid on me. Free from broken friendships that I had continued to carry. I was free because I put the sin on the cross instead of wearing them as a label over my life. During those moments I was running for the Lord and what a beautiful thing it was. God was a genius that day! He used something I loved, like running, to show me how to use it to break out of the mental prison I had been in. After that first hour I wasn't sprinting up the hill anymore because I was so exhausted, but I never once quit. I was exhausted trying to carry the unforgiveness, so I was okay with being physically tired if that's what it took to let my unforgiveness go. Walking out forgiveness God's way changed my life, and I knew His heart was for me to be set free from all anger and unforgiveness.

Forgiveness is hard. The Bible says to forgive 7 times 70 because God knew we couldn't be limited in this area and we would have to be willing to forgive over and over and over. Even when we're exhausted, it's so important to forgive every single part. I didn't just say, "I forgive

Brandon for everything!" I listed out each thing that I had been holding on to and each thing had its own sprint. This is what it looks like to walk out forgiveness. Every time the Enemy tries to tempt you with a thought from the past, you have to choose to forgive again and know that it's not your job to punish the other person. I call the choice of forgiving over and over the hill of forgiveness. The hill of forgiveness is the perfect visual to show me that true forgiveness takes a lot of work and forgiving each part of the pain matters. This first step of forgiveness is key if you truly want to purify your mind from the offense.

The second way God taught me how to forgive was by showing me my desperate need for forgiveness. There was no hill or big story. When I found myself lying flat on a cold bathroom floor in need of God's rescue, that was all it took for me to see that I am no different than anyone who had ever hurt me. I have hurt others in my life, even those whom I love dearly. On that bathroom floor I came face-to-face with the reality of my own humanity. I too, am a sinner who has hurt others. How in the world could I ever choose to not forgive another person after that?

To this day, I keep my heart pure from bitterness. Of course, I have other struggles that I wrestle with, but forgiveness is not one of them. I don't allow myself to have a mental list of hurts that I carry around in my backpack. As I seek forgiveness I am a better wife, mother, daughter, and friend because of it. The gift of forgiveness is the very best gift you can give to someone else and also to yourself.

PROCESS AND REFLECT:

- Before you move on to the next chapter, I encourage you to make a list of the baggage and pain you are carrying. Be specific by naming the hurt, and the person, and every way it has affected you. To be honest, it's going to be really difficult to seek an audience of one in other areas if you can't offer forgiveness to those in your life. Don't rush this crucial chapter, and step towards your growth.

chapter six: fear of man

"Fear of man will prove to be a snare, but whoever trusts in the Lord is kept safe."

PROVERBS 29:25

One of the most crucial parts of learning to seek an audience of one is overcoming the fear of man. About a year ago, I heard a quote during church that said; "It's a very dangerous place to be when we allow external influences to control our inner feelings." There is no better way for me to describe the fear of man than those words "dangerous place to be". Choosing to care so much about what others think is like being at the mercy of other people's opinions. It is not only dangerous, but it puts you in a place of constant insecurity. People's thoughts are inconsistent and they are inaccurate at times. When we allow flawed humans to dictate how we feel about ourselves, we are setting ourselves up for failure and we don't stand a chance.

Since the age of 15, I have had jobs where I felt like I had to worry about what others thought of me. When I was a lifeguard, I was constantly being watched and judged by my performance. I was always "on" because of the importance of the job. As a waitress, I spent every minute trying to make others happy with me and their guest experience. In sales, we all know that if you are not good enough then you lose your job. After college, my first job was a middle school science teacher where all eyes were always on me. As a new teacher I wanted the students to like me and enjoy my class. When I think through all of these jobs, it makes sense that I fell into the trap of wanting to please others.

I know that my people-pleasing behaviors have always been there, but I feel like I really began to fall into this trap when I was leading the women's ministry at my church. My heart for women has always run deep, and at that point in my life I wanted to help as many women as I could. I would say that it went well for a while, but somewhere along the way my mindset changed from pleasing God to pleasing women. It was a slow and deceptive shift, but before I knew it I was making decisions with one question in my head: "Will the women like this and will this make them happy?" It was one thing for me to pick cheesecake for dessert because I thought it would be a crowd pleaser. It's a different ball game when you're fighting what you know God is calling you to do with trying to make everyone happy. In those situations, you can only choose one way—your way or God's way—but I thought I could do both.

The problem with making decisions based on other people's opinions is the fact that it will never be good enough. I realized quickly that there were times I could make 99% of the women happy if I tried really hard, but it would never be 100%. I am not sure why my goal was ever 100%. It seems so ridiculous looking back, but something in me thought that was possible. I continued to spin my wheels, one event after another, only to fall into the same trap, which left me feeling not good enough. I am sure you can guess where that road led. It didn't end well; I found myself completely burnt out and wanting to quit.

The problem with making decisions based on other people's opinions is the fact that it will never be good enough.

It was tough for me to understand how I could have such a burning passion for women's ministry and then be left feeling so defeated and empty inside. It would take years for me to understand those answers, but that couldn't be done until I realized that I had to let go of the fear of man once and for all. My sister had a front row seat to all of this. I was thankful for her wisdom when I asked her about maybe doing another women's event. She looked me dead in the face and said, "Until you do the hard work and seek freedom from the fear of man, you shouldn't ever stand on a stage again." She knew. She saw the unhealthiness. She was the first to see my heart for women and how badly I wanted that ministry back, but she was also the first to see the things in my heart that I needed to abandon. There are times where others can see the unhealth in us easier than we can, so humbling ourselves to hear those hard truths is so important.

Maybe you're thinking to yourself and wondering how fear of man might be playing out in your life. It's different for all of us, but I will tell you that it was hitting me from every direction. It wasn't just with women's ministry. Instagram was certainly a way that the Enemy was creating webs in my mind with this worry. I worried about every little thing I posted because I wanted to make sure I didn't hurt anyone's feelings. I worried when others would post about events that I knew certain friends were not invited to. I would rewrite posts over and over to make sure I wasn't offensive or misleading in any way. I was like a little hamster running on a play wheel, trying to control every part of that app. And guess what? No matter how hard I tried, it was never good enough. It took a while, but I finally began to see that when other people are hurt or offended, it usually goes back to their own insecurities or circumstances in their life. Most of the time, it isn't about me or what I did or didn't post; it's more about them and the health of their mind when they are reading it. It wasn't until I got upset while scrolling on Instagram that it finally clicked, and I understood the root reason why women tend to struggle while viewing social media.

I had been a runner for years and it was something that I loved to do. My love for running was so strong and I would wake up at any hour just to run. Running provided an outlet that set my mind in motion in positive ways. I loved running. I am sure I will get into this more later, but I was diagnosed with rheumatoid arthritis when I was 39, which ultimately stole my ability to run. The disease hit my feet first and it was debilitating. I was devastated because running was so many things for me; it wasn't just a workout. One day I was scrolling on Instagram and came across a post made by a friend showing she had just finished a run. During my running years, I would have seen that post, liked it, and commented on it to encourage her to keep up the good work! However, when I saw the post on this particular day, I didn't leave a comment. I immediately felt a series of emotions fill me. I felt a deep sense of sadness, jealousy, and anger at God because he had allowed this disease to hit me. Please note that none of my emotions or feelings had anything to do with her. She didn't do anything wrong by posting something that made her happy that day. My feelings were about my circumstances. The day I saw her post happened to be a very negative day dealing with my circumstances. I wasn't capable of seeing her post and separating it from my painful situation. Ouch!

Since then, a good friend reminded me that I can't control other people's reactions to my posts, but even more than that, I am not responsible for other people's feelings. It was necessary for me to walk through the pain of viewing a hard post so that I could see that most people's reactions are about them. I have talked to a lot of women about this, and I would say that the majority struggle with social media. Whether you struggle with posting or with viewing, I want you to know that there is freedom from this. Once I accepted my diagnosis and what I had lost because of it, I was able to celebrate others again. I can drive down the road and smile at someone running because I have realized that we all have our own battles to fight. I am fully aware of my battles and I get to choose how I want to fight them. I can accept them and fight them as healthily as I know how, or I can live with a heart of bitterness towards others that are not fighting my same battle.

Later on, we will discuss boundaries and how they helped me navigate my people pleasing tendencies. For now, I want to encourage you to ask God where your heart is when it comes to operating out of fear of man. Are you making decisions based on what He has asked you to do, or are you seeking the approval of others? Are you raising your kids out of the convictions of your heart, or are you giving in so that they will be happy with you? Do you leave church questioning every conversation you had hoping you didn't offend someone? Do you allow other people's opinions to dictate the decisions you make? Does your obedience depend on who is around or who might be watching? Is it hard to stand up for what you believe in because you fear conflict or disharmony? Do your parents, or in-laws, have too much say in your family because you're worried you might offend them? I said before that there were so many layers to the fear of man, but you have to start somewhere. I pray that God will start revealing the areas of your life where you need to redirect your thoughts. It is a battle worth facing.

PROCESS AND REFLECT:

- Before you move forward, maybe list out the things that have become your audience. If we are all honest with ourselves, I promise you will be able to pinpoint what that is for you.
- In what situations do you feel like the little hamster running in circles in an attempt to please someone else?

chapter seven: performance-based love

"For you created my inmost being; you knit me together in my mother's womb. I praise you because I am fearfully and wonderfully made; your works are wonderful, I know that full well."

PSALM 139: 13-14

I have always wanted my family to be proud of me. I remember standing on a stage for a dance recital when I was a little girl. Year after year, that was my favorite part of dance because my parents would watch me and I felt like they were proud of me. I am the eldest child in my family; I have one sister and one brother. I am not sure if it's an eldest child thing or not, but I have always been driven by performance. There is not anything wrong with wanting to perform well in areas of your life, but there were times I found myself performing so that I would feel loved.

We will seek love and attention through negative outlets like social media, inappropriate relationships, or even our clothing.

Remember when I said that love was one of the greatest needs in a woman's heart? I believe this need for love makes it easy to seek love in unhealthy ways. Our need for love makes me think of my kids when they were little. I remember times when it seemed like they were acting out for no apparent reason. After a while I realized that they just needed some attention. As adult women, we have the tendency to do this when it comes to love. We will seek love and attention through negative outlets like social media, inappropriate relationships, or even our clothing. At the same time, we can seek love through positive situations, which fuels our mindset that doing good means others will love us. We start to believe that we will be loved if we perform well. However, seeking love through negative or positive situations can be a trap that leaves us feeling empty.

This performance-based love tends to go well for us until it doesn't. Seeking love from another human will always leave us feeling inadequate. I have been married for 20 years, but my struggle with performance-based love has been one of the biggest lessons that God has taught me through my marriage. Brandon and I have known each other since we were 12 years old. The foundation of our relationship was a very close friendship. It wasn't until our sophomore year of college when we shifted into a romantic relationship. I tell you this because it's important to know that I have loved him for as long as I can remember. There has never been a time when I didn't want him to love me and be proud of me.

As I mentioned before, my first year of college didn't go very well when it came to grades. I was out on my own for the first time and was juggling a new apartment, bills, a job, and a full load of school. I was failing most classes, which was very unusual for me, so Brandon thought it would be fun to give me something to work towards. He told me, "If you can pass your next test, then I will give you a kiss!" To this day, we can't decide who liked the other one first. We had both loved each other as friends for years, but it is still a mystery who started falling for the other one romantically first. I secretly think it was him because of the kiss he motivated me with. I mean, he must have wanted to kiss me if that's the reward he chose, right? He could have chosen anything! After lots of studying, you better believe I passed that test, which led to our first kiss. It was only a peck, but more than that I knew he was proud of me. That mattered to me more than anything. We didn't start dating until over a year later, but that kiss sure went a long way for us both.

Writing this, I think about how sweet it was that I wanted him to be proud of me. I wish I could have kept a healthy boundary with that, but I didn't. My need for him to be proud of me became so overwhelming that I found myself performing in order to get him to love me. Of course, now I know that he has always loved me for just being me, but for a long time there was a lie that would circulate through my thoughts that told me that I wasn't good enough. If I didn't meet his every expectation those thoughts of not being good enough would only get louder. When I made him proud, I felt so loved. When I upset him or failed at normal human things, I felt unloved. Let me tell you, this made for a circus of a marriage for years. My thoughts of not being good enough had nothing to do with him, and everything to do with my inability to understand that he didn't love me based on my performance. However, that lie literally strangled me every time I disappointed him. It wasn't until I failed and he stayed to help me up, that is when I realized I didn't have to earn his love nor could I ever lose it.

Performance-based love is a tricky trap because we think we are doing good things, but our motivation couldn't be more in the wrong place. When we perform for love, our audience becomes the person we are performing for. For me, my audience was Brandon. For you, it may be a parent, a child, a boss, or even a friend that you're trying so hard to impress. Here is a little secret. We will never be good enough for them. We are flawed humans that will disappoint those we love and fall hard at times because our pride sneaks up on us. When our audience is other people, we will always fight the insecurity of never being enough. Not being pretty enough, talented enough, available enough, smart enough, skinny enough, or enough in whatever area you are performing in. It will work very well for you until it doesn't, and that's when you will break.

When we perform for love, our audience becomes the person we are performing for.

I can't tell you how many times I have sat on a bathroom floor and cried because I knew I had disappointed others. I hated that I let others down, but thinking back the flow of tears stemmed from the pain in my heart because I felt unloved. The only good thing was that I was choosing to operate that way. Others were not putting that on me, so I had the choice to get off of that train and let people love me for me. I realized that Brandon could love me and be disappointed with me at the same time. They were not mutually exclusive like the lie I told myself they were. I also realized that I could rest at times and stop trying to do so much in an effort to make sure that my friends around me loved me. I could stop trying to earn love because I knew that the love was already there. It was crazy how much emotional energy it freed up inside of me once I could just be me, flaws and all.

I want to shift gears for a minute because I believe this drive within us to perform in order to feel loved lies much deeper. Scripture is clear when it tells us that we have an enemy whose sole desire is to steal our joy and destroy us from the inside out. Every single day that is the Enemy's number one goal, and every single day it's crucial that we recognize this truth so we can fight the battle well. When we fail to recognize it or call it out, we will find ourselves fighting against the people we love instead of the Enemy himself. We have heard over and over that people are not the enemy, yet many of us spend countless hours fighting the wrong people and the wrong battles. What if we put all of that energy towards fighting the true enemy and protecting our joy at all cost? When I think about myself and how I performed to feel loved, it feels so connected to my joy. If others were happy with me, then I thought I had joy. When I would do a good job, I thought I felt joy. What I didn't realize was that joy was not at all what I felt inside. Instead, it was a temporary happiness that could be lost the minute I let someone down.

When our audience is other people, we will always fight the insecurity of never being enough.

If we want to experience continuous joy, regardless of our circumstances, then we must be aware of the things in our lives that often steal our joy. Before I get into that, I want you to think about how it feels to be stolen from. When I was 16, I found myself being handcuffed in the middle of a grocery store parking lot. My heart was beating out of my chest as the officer told me to walk slowly back into the store. I know some of you are thinking there's no way, but I promise you this is real!

I had just gotten my driver's license, so it was fun to leave the house even if I didn't have a reason to leave. Driving around town was exciting, but that day my sister and I made it a little too exciting. We were driving down Carrier Parkway when my sister had the idea to hit up a grocery store and see what we could steal. She said her and her friends had done it before, and it gave them a rush of excitement. After some convincing, I agreed to go to one store. Three stores later, we found ourselves sitting in my car, experiencing the rush of emotions, and thinking just one more store! My trunk was filled with hair ties, candy, and nail polish—nothing we truly needed—but there was something inside of us that made us want to do it one more time. So, we did just that.

Unfortunately, the last store that we chose just so happened to have undercover cops working that day who were watching all of the action taking place on the aisles. Before I knew it, we saw the cops coming after us. We started walking faster towards my car. My sister yelled at me to run, but I knew that I wouldn't be fast enough. With no other option, I stopped in the middle of the parking lot with my hands behind my back. It was the absolute worst feeling in the world.

Recently, my kids asked me if I had ever stolen anything. By the way, I really dislike these types of questions. I have vowed to always tell them the truth, but it really sucks when the truth is hard to say. Anyways, as I began to tell them the story, I couldn't help but think about how it felt to steal and also how it feels to be stolen from. In a weird way, I can see the Enemy getting such a rush when he attempts to steal our joy and we fall right into the trap. I picture him hitting us in the same area over and over because he knows that it works on us. He is not smart, and sadly all he has to do is get in our head with the same few thoughts and we go down without even swinging.

This makes me so angry when I think about it happening to myself, but I get even angrier when I see him trying to take my children down with his lies. Talk about a whole new level of anger when that mama bear comes out! What's crazy is that I can so easily recognize when it's happening to my kids, but when the attacks are on me, it seems like I am falling before I can even catch my breath. What does this look like? Well, we all struggle with different things that try to steal our joy, but let me give you some ideas to help you identify yours. I suggest highlighting the ones that you struggle with.

- Perfectionism
- Insecurities about our body, our intelligence, or our past
- Loss
- Jealousy
- Pain or sickness
- Unforgiveness
- Worry
- Worrying about what others think of you
- Busyness
- Not being good enough
- Frustration and anger
- Fear of missing out
- Situations you can't control or dealing with people you can't control
- Social media
- Conflict

- Fear in general
- Bitterness or memories from the past
- Aging and body changes
- Watching our children struggle
- Not feeling seen or heard
- Distractions
- School and jobs
- Comparison

If I am being honest, I would say that I have dealt with every single one of these at some point in my life. However, a few of these are so sensitive to me. All it takes is one strike to my thoughts and I will crumble if I am not armored up for the battle. After 44 years, I have learned what these weaknesses are and how to see them coming so that I can be successful in keeping the Enemy from stealing my joy. When I think about this chapter as a whole, so many of the things on this list are rooted in our need to be loved or our need for approval in some way. One way or another, it seems to always circle back to us performing in order to feel loved or good enough. This behavior is beyond toxic, and it will trickle down to our children and seep into the relationships that are most important to us. So, what do we do?

1. IDENTIFY YOUR TOP FIVE

What steals your joy? What takes your breath away, gets you off track, or throws your day off in a way that is hard to recover from?

2. GET ANGRY ABOUT IT AND MAKE THE CONSCIOUS DECISION TO FIGHT THE CORRECT ENEMY

Remember when I asked you how it feels to be stolen from? It feels terrible and leaves us feeling exposed. The Enemy is stealing from us, and it's time to let a righteous anger fuel us to fight. If you get mad at another female on social media, don't allow yourself to form a hate for her. Remind yourself that the root of your anger is comparison, jealousy, or maybe anger at her behaviors. Ultimately, the Devil is the one tempting you to put your anger towards her because he knows that will cause gossip and division! Instead of falling into that trap, take those yucky feelings and ask God to show you how to deal with them and move past them. It's not beneficial to stay stuck in the social media reel of emotions, trust me! It should make us angry when he tells us we are not a good mom or a good wife. We should be furious when he throws our past in our faces when we have already claimed the blood of Jesus over that sin. These are just a few examples, but each of the things on the list has a root and there is truth that can be spoken over each of them.

3. CHOOSE WHAT IS TRUE OVER THE LIE YOUR HEAD MIGHT BE TELLING YOU.

Students, if school is overwhelming, then take a breath and remind yourself that your grades do not define you. Moms, if you feel like you're failing when you put yourself up against other moms, speak truth over that thought. God gave you those babies, and He has trusted you and only you with those children. Cling to that, grow in that, seek forgiveness when you fall, and pursue those babies with all your heart. You were chosen for this! I remember looking at the skin on my stomach years ago and wishing it was tighter. Then Brandon said, "When I see your stomach, I think about how that stomach carried all four of our babies." He didn't see the imperfections in the way I saw them, and his perspective allowed me to see something new. I struggle tremendously with things I cannot control. Sometimes, just saying that out loud and telling myself that I can only control my behavior is all I need to stop the chaos in my head. Find what is true about your triggers and fight the battle well.

4. DON'T FORGET THAT THE ENEMY DOESN'T TAKE A DAY OFF IN HIS ATTEMPTS TO LIE TO US OR DESTROY OUR LIVES.

Special occasions, vacations, or any other day is not off limits to him. I have learned this lesson the hard way. If I don't pursue Jesus every single day, then I leave my mind vulnerable to those attacks. Stay in the word, keep your worship music going, pray throughout the day, and keep your eyes wide open. The Bible says to be sober minded and not distracted by the things of this world, and I believe this is why. The Enemy will use anything to get us off track!

I know there are a few of you wondering what happened after my sister and I were handcuffed that day. We did the walk of shame across the store and sat until our mom came to pick us up. I have never seen her so angry or disappointed in my life. We spent the summer doing community service hours at a children's therapy center where we cleaned toys and other things around the office. I learned my lesson and never stole again, but more importantly, I learned that the rush of emotion is never worth the consequences.

I encourage you to spend some time on this chapter. When we allow our joy to be stolen, it usually means we lose things in our life we hold valuable. We can't sacrifice what is valuable to us by choosing to go down without a fight. Don't forget that temporary happiness found in our good performances is not the same as joy. Jesus is the only giver of joy, and it has nothing to do with how good we are or how we perform. Operating daily with this performance-based love is telling God we don't believe His love for us enough, but choosing an audience of one is believing in the gift of Christ's unconditional love for us. Fight for healthy thoughts, fight for your family, and fight for your joy because all of these are worth fighting for! Lastly, choose to believe that you are loved because you are a child of God. That kind of love cannot be earned nor can it be lost.

PROCESS AND REFLECT:

- Look back at the list of ideas as far as things that might steal your joy. What would your top 5 biggest struggles be? (Remember, this is step one in walking through this chapter.)

chapter eight: boundaries

"Look carefully at how you walk, not as unwise but as wise, making the best use of the time, because the days are evil. Therefore do not be foolish, but understand what the will of the Lord is."

EPHESIANS 5:15-17

Ever since I can remember, I have had an unhealthy relationship with food. Growing up, I struggled with my weight and never figured out how to put healthy boundaries in place. For the most part, I fought through it and made my way through high school without letting it control me, but my first year of college was a different ball game. I was staying up late and eating Taco Bell while studying for tests. Before I knew it, I had gained over 40 pounds. I knew it was an addiction when I started hiding while I ate. I can specifically remember hiding in a closet to eat a Snickers bar and driving to a parking lot to eat two fast food meals alone. You wouldn't think that food was so bad of an addiction, but it was. It left me feeling so shameful inside. The deceit of it was the same as any other addiction, I didn't want anyone to know how bad it was.

I was able to get through the fall semester of sophomore year without completely melting down, but I didn't get further than that. I remember packing up for Christmas break and telling my roommate, Robyn, that I wouldn't be coming back to our room for the spring semester. Robyn was such a light in my life. She was beautiful, inside and out, and her dedication in life was something I longed for. She would wake up each day to exercise, she knew what boundaries with food looked like, and she was always filled with so much joy. She loved Jesus, and I knew that she had a freedom that I didn't understand at the time. Meanwhile, I was just a 19-year-old who felt more lost and insecure than ever.

As much as I loved her, I knew that I couldn't continue living with her because of my weight and the toll it was taking on me emotionally. If I am being honest, it was hard to live with someone who had all the things that I wanted. She was fit, she was healthy minded, and she exhibited a self-control in her life that was rare. It wasn't just with food; she had self-control to read the Bible, exercise, and keep a strong dedication to her schoolwork. After I packed up for the break, I remember sitting on my bed and telling her the truth. I felt fat, I felt sad, I felt insecure, and it was too hard to be her roommate. I told her that I loved her, but I didn't know how to separate it all.

I wasn't prepared for her response when I told her the truth, but it changed the direction of my life forever. To this day, I know that her response came from a place of finding her security in the right places, which was why she lived life with such joy. She heard my insecurities and embraced them by choosing to help me. She asked me to give it one more semester and to trust her. All I had to do was wake up each day and follow her through her routine in an effort to get to a healthier place in several areas of my life. Three and a half months later, I lost 25 pounds, which definitely helped me mentally, but what I gained through those months was an understanding of boundaries.

If we want to be our best, we have to surround ourselves with healthy influences and create boundaries to help us get there.

I began to learn that food wasn't bad, but several servings of food at a time was bad for my body. I began to see that boundaries weren't necessarily negative, but they were a way to actually keep negative things from happening. For some reason, I had always viewed boundaries inaccurately, which ultimately led to a lack of boundaries. I also learned that if someone has something in their life that I want, like a characteristic, then the best way to grow in that area is to model them and their behaviors. Women often see other women as intimidating. Even if they want to be like them, they often push them away, succumb to jealousy, and build walls. It doesn't make any sense, but I think the majority of women behave this way. I love the quote that says, "Jealousy will have you gossiping about a person you should be learning from." What if we chose to stop the jealousy in our minds and learn from each other? What if we leaned

Boundaries are worth setting because our hearts are worth protecting.

into those that intimidate us? I promise we will grow so much and realize that they are human just like us, only they have already walked through that part of their journey. If we want to be our best, we have to surround ourselves with healthy influences and create boundaries to help us get there.

Remember when I wrote about Instagram and how there was a time when it was difficult for me to scroll past posts where women were running? Through that hard time, I set a boundary. I hid those posts until I was able to get to a healthier place with it. I could have easily continued to look at them, but it was eating away at me every time and making it impossible for me to get back on my feet. I have often given this advice to women, yet many still choose to look at social media because they fear they will be out of the loop. Choosing to not set a boundary when you know it is what's best for you is choosing to stay stuck. We will never move forward if we are unwilling to do what it takes to get unstuck.

Choosing to not set a boundary when you know it is what's best for you is choosing to stay stuck.

Luckily, our children have boundaries that are good for them. If they cross them, they are usually not life altering. Unfortunately, as adults, there are boundaries that we cross that have lasting impacts on our lives. I don't think it would take long for most of us to think back to a time when we crossed a big boundary and remember the emotional wreckage that it left because life is full of baggage and wreckage. What if you could learn to put proper boundaries in place so that you could protect yourself, your thoughts, your marriage, and your friendships in such a way that they would flourish? What if we could learn how to truly stay in our lane so that we could avoid getting involved in situations that are only going to negatively fuel us throughout our day? Boundaries are worth setting because our hearts are worth protecting.

Instagram is just a small, simple boundary, but many of us would benefit from relationship boundaries, work-related boundaries, food boundaries, screen time boundaries, and even boundaries with our time. I can't tell you how many times I have fallen into bed completely exhausted because I had no idea how to say, "No, I am so sorry, but I can't make that happen today." Something as simple as the inability to say no had me going in circles, a.k.a people pleasing, and the people closest to me were the ones that would suffer. For you, maybe it is a boundary in your friendships and deciding to never talk bad about your friend to another person. Whatever the case, boundaries keep us from piling on pain that doesn't have to be there.

A lack of personal boundaries usually results in regret, and regret leads to taking our eyes off the right audience and putting them on our pain, shame, and the wreckage. I wish I could say that I learned how to put boundaries in place after that year of college. I found success when it came to my relationship with food, but it didn't take long before I realized that boundaries were necessary in every area of my life. I needed boundaries to protect my marriage and my home. Brandon and I realized quickly how boundaries were crucial when it came to our children, sleepovers at other houses, and deciding who we felt comfortable with them spending time with. So many times I would forget that I needed boundaries with my time so I would overcommit and be left feeling exhausted. Psalms 39:1 encourages us to guard our words, because our thoughts and our mouths need boundaries so that we don't use either of them in a destructive way. I hate to say it, but the only way I learned how to do this was by failure. To this day, we have a saying in our house to grab our attention when someone needs to check themselves. Whether it's Brandon, myself, or one of the kids, any time someone starts to worry about someone else we say, "Stay in your lane!" We have slowly tried to teach them that getting out of their lane, or crossing a boundary, only leads to bigger issues.

Learning to set boundaries is a process, but each time you do it, you will see that it brings so much freedom. Boundaries allow us to do what makes us comfortable because they protect us from the things that will make us uncomfortable. Whether it is setting an end time for the playdate so you don't have people at your house all day long or setting a boundary with the person in your life that has too much access to your emotions. I promise you will find freedom when you establish boundaries. Changing our habits or removing a temptation can sometimes be all that we need to find our win for the moment. Little boundaries create so much space to breathe, so don't be afraid to look at where the majority of your stress is coming from and set up a small boundary. Yes, there may be others in your life that don't understand it at first because it is different, but they will adjust and you will be a better friend because of it. Remember to continue adopting the mindset of pleasing God over man, especially when you are having to set more difficult boundaries!

As my girls get older, I see how crucial my parenting is when it comes to teaching my girls about boundaries with friendships, dating, and decisions they will make along the way. I can either shy away from those conversations or I can teach them how to set healthy boundaries to hopefully avoid much of the wreckage that I had to sort through growing up. There are three parenting thoughts I wanted to share when it comes to boundaries.

1. I AM SLOWLY LEARNING THAT PARENTING WITH BOUNDARIES FEELS HEALTHIER THAN CONSTANTLY SETTING RULES WHEN I AM NOT EVEN SURE THERE NEEDS TO BE A RULE

From what I am seeing, setting a boundary allows kids to slowly grow up without them feeling like I am trying to control them. Our goal as parents is to consistently guide the baby steps until they leave our home. I want them to feel confident in setting boundaries in all areas when that time comes.

2. BOUNDARIES ALLOW FOR MOVEMENT

Sometimes the rule is just yes or no, black or white. Other times, boundaries can be adjusted as they grow up and are ready for a little more freedom. It might sound silly but when Brylee turned 15, Brandon said she could have Instagram with a 15-minute daily time limit. It seems like a tight boundary, but he doesn't want her having endless time on something that could potentially affect her emotions or self-worth. Over time, this boundary can be adjusted, but this was his way of saying yes without having to go all in.

3. IT'S SO IMPORTANT TO RESPECT OTHER PEOPLE'S BOUNDARIES, THEIR PARENTING, AND THEIR HOMES

My sister-in-law, Ali, does not like to be touched or to have anyone in her personal space. Our family was the complete opposite. We love to hug or sit so close to each other that we are almost using each other as a pillow, ha! Even after all these years we still laugh about it, or purposely sit close to Ali just to see how she will react. It's all in fun, but over the years we have both had to recognize one another's boundary and decide whether or not to respect it. Anytime someone operates differently than us, it is important that we check our hearts on the issue. The issue could be a smaller thing, like personal space, or a much more serious issue with big implications. All of us have a tendency to make judgments on others when we don't agree or maybe when we don't understand the why behind it. As natural as this is, these judgements cause us to go out of bounds, which usually leads to conflict or being a poor role model for our kids. At the end of the day, your child is ultimately your responsibility, while other kids belong to someone else. Plus, every child and every home is different. I am raising four kids in the same home, but I guarantee you there will be times where their boundaries may look different. Their needs are not the same, the way they react is not the same, and the way they interact is not the same, which is why their boundaries won't be the same. It's easier said than done, but doing your best to focus on your own home and your children will relieve you from additional emotions that you don't have to carry.

Healthy boundaries keep our eyes on God instead of the mess we made without them.

It is important to set the boundary before you are in the situation when it's needed because that will set you up to be more successful. Before we are faced with situations, we tend to be able to think more logically, which can help us make clear plans for when we are faced with a decision down the line. When we wait until we are in the moment, our emotions tend to take over, which usually overrides our logical thinking. I am sure if I asked you to think of one area where you could use a boundary, it wouldn't be hard to come up with something. Many of you might share the similar food battle that I face. Maybe it's wine, social media, relational boundaries, or boundaries in your thoughts; the list is endless. You would be surprised at how little changes lead to big outcomes. Healthy boundaries keep our eyes on God instead of the mess we made without them.

PROCESS AND REFLECT:

- Where do you struggle with setting boundaries in your life? Try to identify "why you struggle" with each of them. (fear of their reaction or maybe trying to avoid conflict.)
- Do you feel you are healthy minded when it comes to social media? Is there a small boundary you could set to help you be more successful in this?
- Are there specific people in your life where you know you need a boundary but haven't set one yet (in-laws, a coworker, a friend)?

chapter nine: a blurry lens

"For God is not a God of confusion but of peace."

1 CORINTHIANS 14:33

When I was a little girl, my mom and dad took me through a car wash. You know the kind that goes through a tunnel with all the spinning and loud noises? You're basically trapped inside with no way out. I am not sure if I really remember this like I think I do or if I have just heard the story enough times to trick my brain into thinking I actually remember it. Either way, my mom will tell you that as we drove through the car wash that day I completely freaked out and screamed the whole way through it. I am sure my parents didn't know what to do with me, so they just watched it all happen until it was over. What other choice did they have? It must have been traumatic because I am 43 years old and I still have to keep some Xanax close by when I pull into one of those things.

I recently drove through one and tried to process how the carwash works while I went through it. I wanted to overcome the fear of it, and understanding how things work helps me with fear. I took a deep breath and slowly started rolling on the tracks. I wasn't prepared for what happened next, but I love how cool God is. He knew He had my attention, and He immediately started speaking to my heart. He showed me that the reason I was so fearful was because I wasn't looking through a clear lens in that tunnel. It was soapy, it was chaotic and loud, it felt confusing seeing all the wipers go in every direction, and I felt trapped. None of those things feel good, especially when you are not in control of removing yourself from the situation. When I was stuck in that tunnel, I realized that my tendency was to panic and allow thoughts of anxiety to win. All I wanted was for the soap to be cleaned off the window just a little bit so that I could see to the other side.

I can't help but think about how many of us women feel so many of the same things as we are trying to walk through life. The lens we are looking through is blurry for a number of reasons, which means we are all trying to make logical and healthy decisions without a clear mind. Living life with a blurry lens is a recipe for a disaster, yet we wonder why relationships and situations around us are so messy!

I see this play out most commonly in female friendships. It doesn't matter if they are 13-year-old girls or 40-year-old women, a blurry lens is a blurry lens. Abuse, abandonment, addictions, sickness, loss, anxiety, divorce, and betrayal are some of the reasons why we have a blurry lens. So much of our pain started as young kids, and we hold onto it throughout our lives. We walk into friendships, marriages, and parenthood with a blurry lens and as life continues to happen, our lenses only fog up more. Yes, there are some women that deal with their pain in a healthy way, but I have seen that to be rare. I would say that the majority of us are carrying around our pain as if it is a part of us. Our grip on it is so tight that we appear as if we don't want to let it go. The hardest part about all of it is that all of our lenses are blurry for different reasons. It would be much easier to understand one another if we all had the same soapy lens for the exact same reasons, but that is usually not the case.

Years ago, I was celebrating a birthday with a group of women. This was during the time I was in ministry, so I was very aware of situations going on inside many of the women's lives in the group. Each woman came to the table with a different pair of "glasses" on. Of course, we all got to the table, dressed nice with smiles on, but there was so much hiding behind those smiles. Let's just go ahead and use me as an example. I sat down at the table that night and was looking through a lens of insecurity since this was during my heightened years of people pleasing. I saw soap suds of unforgiveness for one of the women at the table. I was in the middle of battling food again, so I felt uncomfortable in my clothes, which made me look at other women at the table with a jealous heart. I was sleep deprived because I had very small children, so my brain was foggy. I knew that two of the women at the table didn't get along well, so I was trying to control conversations to keep the peace. This list was endless.

I sat down and looked fine, but the lenses I was looking through were such a mess that my reality of that dinner looked very different from the others sitting around me. I also remember the topic of marriage coming up. This automatically stressed me out because I had recently counseled several of the women at the table. I knew that their marriages were on the rocks, so I immediately feared what would be said. One of the women started talking about how happy she was in her marriage while I was sitting next to a woman who had just found out that her husband had a pornography addiction. Her lens was negative about marriage, yet she was trying to smile while listening to others talk about their happy marriages. You see where I am going with this? When our lens is clouded, we have to try to overcome our own mental challenges while doing life, getting along with others, and celebrating one another. This leads to stored up anger, misunderstandings, jealousy, and withdrawing from others because we don't know how to appropriately deal with our pain.

When our lens is clouded, we have to try to overcome our own mental challenges while doing life, getting along with others, and celebrating one another.

I can't help but think back to the old Tanna and the thick clouded lenses she was attempting to live life with. There was a time when it was so blurry that I am not even sure how she got through the day. Imagine all of this inside your head at once and then imagine trying to build a marriage and a ministry with this foundation. Extreme anxiety, an abnormal sensitivity to weight, never feeling good enough, suicidal thoughts, pain of addiction, fear of failure, a perfectionist mindset and a secret battle with depression. Talk about a disaster waiting to happen and yet that was my life for so many years.

Sin, either our sin or someone else's sin, is the ultimate root of why our imaginary glasses get blurry. Our own sin clouds our lenses because when we sin it leads to shame, guilt, regret, and many emotions that make life harder on us. We are waking up every day trying to start fresh, but our feet are still planted in the past, which creates a constant blurry lens. So many of us are straddling between doing right and doing wrong, living God's way and living our way. That in itself is sin, not to mention extremely confusing for our mind. When our mind is confused, it creates a fog. On the flip side, when it is someone else's sin that was done towards us, it can lead to bitterness, anger, unforgiveness, and sadness. Carrying these negative emotions will also cause our lens to become clouded. The pain and memory of it all pushes us down, which drains us daily. Again, more of a blurry lens, and we wonder why anxiety levels are through the roof.

Sin, either our sin or someone else's sin, is the ultimate root of why our imaginary glasses get blurry.

Unfortunately, many of us are carrying both our own sin as well as the yucky fruit caused by the hurts of others. This is why I believe sin is often the root of a blurry lens. The only way to walk through life seeing clearly is to make things right in your own heart on both sides of it. We must flee from sin daily, not even allowing that door to open because an open door leads to a big trap. Secondly, we must deal with the pain in our hearts. I can remember women telling me over and over that they are too scared to even try counseling in an attempt to deal with their pain because they are not sure what all will come out of them. I always understood their hearts when they would say this, but through my own journey I have seen that what is inside of me is going to come out whether I choose to deal with it or not. It can come out in a healthy way, like through counseling, or it can come out in very ugly ways at the wrong times.

I hate to tell you this, but you're not doing yourselves any favors by running from your pain. More than likely, you're hurting others along the way because you are unwilling to deal with your own pain.

Walking through conflict with someone you love can be really difficult unless you are both looking through a clear lens. This is because we all have the tendency to bring our baggage into conversations about conflict. It's like we can't help it. Have you ever been arguing with your spouse and then all the sudden something comes out of your mouth from like five years ago? I remember doing this for years. I never understood why I did that until I realized I hadn't forgiven Brandon, so past pain would naturally come up as if it had happened that day. I hated doing it because it always ended with me feeling so defeated. It's crazy when you think about it, but I have to wonder how many of us are still stuck in that cycle and are in need of a clear lens! Choosing to deal with it will be a very hard, rocky road, but man it is pure freedom when the day finally comes where you get to walk in purity and peace. There is no greater feeling, friends. I would say it is so worth it!

Walking through conflict with someone you love can be really difficult unless you are both looking through a clear lens.

I love going back to a passage in Chapter Six of Romans where it reminds us that sin cannot conquer us if we are in Christ Jesus. For years, I thought I was in Christ and walking with Him, but that was so far from the truth. Walking with Him means waking up every day and choosing Him—choosing to communicate with Him through prayer, choosing to know Him more through reading the Word, and choosing to worship Him throughout the day in your car or in your home. Yes, maybe I was a Christian, but I wasn't in Christ daily. The Bible does say that sin cannot conquer us, but we have to be walking in the Spirit daily with Him.

Living with a blurry lens is your choice. It is no one else's, just yours. No one else can take the steps to deal with your sin. No one else can forgive and start walking through your pain to pursue healing. No else can open your Bible and read it for you. I didn't like hearing this, but my blurry lens was my responsibility. I tried to blame others for years because I was the one hurting, but it only made my life and brain more clouded than ever. Is your lens dirty? Do you feel like I did as a little girl going through that car wash in a panic, feeling so confused because you can't see through the soap suds and mess that have piled up? If so, I want clarity for you! Let's do the work once and for all!

PROCESS AND REFLECT:

- Ask God to show you all the ways your lens is blurry. I would also suggest asking a trusted friend or family member to speak into this as well. This is a humbling process but you will see God's power when you humble yourself before Him. Sometimes we have to go back many years to sort through all the baggage we are carrying. I encourage you to make a list of what is revealed, because it's hard to deal with something that we haven't identified. Make a list so you can see what you're dealing with.
- Choose one thing on the list and begin to ask God to heal it. Starting with one thing will allow you to truly deal with that one thing before moving to the next. Some things on your list will take more time, and maybe even counseling, but give yourself grace because it's not an easy journey. Here's the thing, getting to the root of the issue is so important. Brandon

is a dentist and when he does a root canal he will tell you how important it is to clean out every part of every root before closing it up. If he only cleans out "most of the root" then it might feel better for a while but the pain will eventually come back. Dig deep and walk through each part before moving to the next thing.

- Surround yourself with others who are walking with the Lord. Accountability is so helpful for several reasons, but especially when you feel yourself going backwards. We need friends who are going to help us stay on track towards healing and not lead us astray.

10

chapter ten: loss

"Even though I walk through the darkest valley, I will fear no evil, for you are with me; your rod and your staff, they comfort me."

PSALM 23:4

My third daughter, Audree Ann, is 12 years old now, but when she was two years old we experienced something that, even today, still hurts my heart to think about. Every Fourth of July, our family would travel to a place called Lost Pines to celebrate. It was a small family resort in Texas that had become such a sweet tradition for us. Each year was filled with beautiful memories and more red, white, and blue than you can imagine. This particular year, I was eight months pregnant with Heath and the girls were two, four, and six. To say that we had our hands full was an understatement! Audree couldn't swim yet, so all day she had been prancing around in her stars and stripes ruffle swimsuit with her pink floaties on. I can close my eyes and remember it perfectly. All five of us were playing by the sand, wading in shallow water, and enjoying the music when I looked up and saw that Audree was gone.

I didn't panic right away because it was a very safe place with only families, but then I looked over to the right and saw her pink floaties on the ground by the sandcastle she had been building. At that moment, my heart started beating out of my chest as I pictured the water park and all of the areas with deeper water. Brandon and I both looked at each other and knew that we needed to find her quickly, so we both started running and yelling her name all over that place. After looking in all of the spots she liked to play in, I think we both hit another level of fear knowing that we were running out of time if she had gone into the water. My best guess is that we searched for about five or six minutes across the dry land before I found myself kneeling in the sand because I couldn't breathe. I was so very pregnant and all the running was too much. I collapsed in the sand weeping hysterically.

All I could think was that she was somewhere under the water and that I would never see her alive again. It makes me physically sick to think about it now because of how real and traumatic it was. By this point, there were so many people helping and searching for Audree as well as staff helping me as I was having a panic attack on the ground. When I looked up, I saw something I will never forget. Brandon came running over the bridge with my precious little girl in her ruffle skirt. He found her. She had made her way to the other side of the resort and was standing near the lazy river. Once I realized she was safe, I cried even harder, but this time it was with tears of thankfulness.

Loss has a way of abruptly entering our hearts in such a way that we experience every emotion at a level of intensity that is new to us.

Once we had made it back to the room a few hours later, I found myself leaning up against the wall in the shower crying uncontrollably. At that point she was fine, but my emotions had to catch up with that reality. Audree was lost only temporarily and yet everything that unfolded inside of me was extremely intense. Loss has a way of abruptly entering our hearts in such a way that we experience every emotion at a level of intensity that is new to us. Just when we feel like we're finally catching our breath, all it takes is a memory, a picture on social media, or a similar situation before we feel like we are suffocating all over again. It is a vicious cycle that I wouldn't wish on anyone, but at the end of the day we are all going to walk through a loss. Therefore, it is important to learn how to walk through it well. Loss of any kind changes us, but it doesn't have to ruin us.

One of my very dear friends, Courtney, lost a child. God allowed me to be one of the people to walk closely with her through that difficult time. As hard as it was, it was a gift to be able to listen, to love, and to learn with her over the last 10 years. We have spent countless hours learning what it looks like to lose something so precious and cling to Jesus all at the same time. I got to be there when the hard times were suffocating her, and I got to celebrate with her when God would move in her life despite the excruciating pain. I say it was a gift because

Loss of any kind changes us, but it doesn't have to ruin us.

Courtney's journey slowly taught me that the only way to walk through loss in a healthy way is to walk through each part of it well. Pushing the feelings aside or trying to put the memories in a box creates a buildup that usually leads to an explosion. I said before that loss will change us, but it doesn't have to ruin us. I have learned that walking through each part of the loss well enables us to heal even the tiniest threads that are connected to the loss. Loss has so many layers, sometimes ones we don't even see. Understanding every layer is important if we desire true healing. Healing doesn't always mean forgetting, but healing does mean being able to tear down the wall of anger that the loss built up inside of us.

I have learned that walking through each part of the loss well enables us to heal even the tiniest threads that are connected to the loss.

When I started writing this chapter, I had to take a long break because I didn't feel qualified to share my heart on loss. I see now that I was feeling insecure because I felt like the loss I had experienced might not be "big enough" in the eyes of others to be taken seriously. Sure, I had felt loss, but I was carrying some sort of guilt inside of me because others around me had experienced a more difficult or traumatic loss. Since I watched friends lose children, which in my mind would be unbearable, somewhere along the way the Enemy had told me that any loss that I was feeling wasn't important because it wasn't as bad as their loss. Sometimes we carry around thoughts and ideas that shape the way we go through life that are so far from accurate. It's almost scary thinking about the times I have grabbed onto a thought and owned it as if I had read it in the Bible. No, I have never lost a child, but there are many areas where loss has left a lasting impact on me. I realized that comparing loss was only stopping me from dealing with the unhealth in my heart that was related to loss.

I want to switch directions for a minute. You may be reading this right now and say that you haven't faced the loss of a child. Many would agree that they can't relate to that, so it is important that I share this next part with you. There have been times in my life where I didn't deal with loss or sadness appropriately because it didn't fit the mold of what I thought great loss should look like. I thought I could only let myself grieve if the loss was big enough. Loss of a loved one is inevitable, but loss hits all of our lives in all shapes and sizes.

When I was 30 years old, I began a women's boot camp in my backyard. I would say that we had about eight of us that first summer. We would meet early in the morning to exercise. I looked forward to that time so much because I loved connecting with other women in that setting. We would laugh, we would share, we would sweat, and over time we began building some really neat friendships. Each summer we would start it up again, and each year our group grew larger. People would move and new friends would come, but the heart of the morning always remained the same. I began to add a devotional time to the workout, and before we knew it, God was using that time together in a special way to grow all of us spiritually. Summer boot camps became such an important part of my life. Each woman held a place in my heart that only had her name on it, and my life felt so spiritually fruitful during those years.

Towards the end of the summer of 2018, my mornings changed forever. I woke up to an early alarm so that I could get to boot camp, but on this particular day I wasn't able to walk. The pain in my feet was excruciating and every step took so much effort. I hate thinking back to that day because it was that day when I lost something I loved. Within a few weeks, I was diagnosed with rheumatoid arthritis. The disease initially hit my hands and feet, which was why I was struggling to walk. Most mornings I would find myself crawling or limping to the bathroom, and it didn't take long for me to fully understand the reality of the diagnosis. It sucked so badly. The diagnosis was awful because I was told it would only get worse over time. There were things

I had to let go of because I lost so much of the function in my feet for quite some time. I not only lost the function in my feet, but I lost my mornings with these women, which led me into a hard season of isolation. I lost the time with them, I lost the conversations, I lost the spiritual touches that would happen in the middle of leading those devotionals, and I felt like I lost those friendships. No, no one in my life had died, but it felt like something inside of me died when I received the diagnosis. Loss is defined as grieving something that is valuable to you. My feet were valuable to me; therefore, this was a loss that needed to be grieved appropriately.

Loss is defined as grieving something that is valuable to you.

How does loss circle back to learning to have an audience of one? Typically when we lose something or someone, all we can do is focus on the pain of the loss and not on the power of Jesus. We are human and so much of our reaction is natural, but when we choose to not grieve God's way then we eventually find ourselves stuck in an unhealthy mindset for months or years at a time. When we grieve without God, we begin to make decisions or accusations of others that stem from our unhealthy way of thinking instead of through the clear lens that God desires for us. The longer we stay stuck in our loss, the more we throw the door wide open for the Enemy to entangle every part of our lives with the pain.

It's so important to have someone around you that can tell you the truth and tell you the hard things that most people can't get away with. The close people in our lives can see things more clearly when we are the ones in the muddy water, so we have to not only look to them for truth, but we need to be able to count on them for that truth. Yes, of course we need to look to Jesus, but there are times we need someone that loves us to look us straight in the eyes and say, "Stop! You're making this worse for yourself!" Grief causes our lenses to be very clouded, so we have to humble ourselves in order to listen to those looking in through a clear lens. We must choose to not be defensive, knowing that we trust what they are saying is for our own good. Walking through grief is like riding a giant roller coaster with a blindfold on. The unknown in itself is frightful and not being able to see when it is going to hit you next leaves you vulnerable.

Maybe you're reading this today and you need to be the one to look someone you love in the face and tell them the truth. I encourage you to do that when God opens the door. Just remember, you haven't earned the right to give the hard truth to just anyone. It takes time to build this kind of foundation and requires a special trust between the two of you. I have also learned that timing and delivery are key. If you ask God to open the door, you will feel it when it's time because the Holy Spirit will overwhelm you inside. With God's timing and His heart of a gracious delivery, I believe that any relationship can do this well and grow closer through it. Whether it's your spouse, a family member, or a friend, I promise you, it's worth the work for someone you love.

Our attention needs to be on the things above us, not on the things behind us. Stopping every hour to look backwards will slow us down and tempt us to relive the same pain over and over in our minds. It's not good for anyone, so why not let yourself feel the pain in a healthy way by setting boundaries so that you can slowly learn to grieve God's way? Feel it, talk through it, yell through it, worship through it, cry through it, and when you're ready, accept it. I remember the day I told myself, "This is your new normal. You have an autoimmune disease that does not have a cure. You get to choose how you want to walk through it." I didn't hate the situation any less, but I made the choice that I was going to walk the journey as well as I could. Instead of staying stuck and bitter inside, I decided to accept the cards I had been dealt and play the best hand I could with the things I could control.

Always remember, it's never wise to compare grief. What is valuable to one person may not be as valuable to another; therefore, loss will hit all of us differently. The moment I learned that I was responsible for grieving the losses in my own heart, was the day I was able to shift my eyes from my pain and start taking steps forward. Loss is a part of life that each of us will face, but we always have a choice in how we will walk through it.

You might be wondering, "What does it look like to grieve God's way versus stuffing it inside and staying bitter?" I am no expert, but there were a few things God taught me through my loss that I want to share with you.

1. DON'T FIGHT THE PAIN

Loss is so very difficult and regardless of our personality, or emotional capacity, our hearts need to be allowed to feel all of it. Let yourself cry, scream, vent and allow yourself to be human. As moms, I know there are times we try to be strong for our children in these moments, but it's important that they see us grieve well because they too will walk through pain one day. God wants us to communicate with Him, even in our anger, because transparency will lead to intimacy. Oftentimes our pride wants to tell everyone we are fine, but it's so much harder for God to strengthen us in our weakness if we don't humble ourselves with honesty.

2. ACCEPT THE REALITY OF YOUR SITUATION

It took months for me to finally accept my rheumatoid arthritis diagnosis, but God was able to show me my next step once I did. Denial felt like a bad dream that I kept waking up to, but accepting it gave me clarity to see in front of me. Clarity is so important so that we can hear the Holy Spirit and see God moving. I needed to see that God could use me despite my circumstances, therefore I had to accept my new reality.

3. GROW FROM YOUR PAIN

After years of experiencing different levels of pain, I have come to believe that the only thing that makes my pain worth it is to see how God changes me through it. Whether we chose the loss, and it's a consequence of our sin, or the pain simply happened to us, God can use it all to grow us. I understand it's difficult to pray for this when you're hurting, but I assure you that it will bring meaning to loss if you pursue the Lord . Asking God, "What do you want to show me through this pain?" or "What needs to be chiseled in my heart?", will create in you a heart of humility, which leads to growth

PROCESS AND REFLECT:

- What things have you lost that are causing you to experience pain? Small things and big things. (someone's trust, something physical, someone you love, etc)
- Is the way you are grieving, or not grieving, affecting other areas in your life?
  If so, describe.

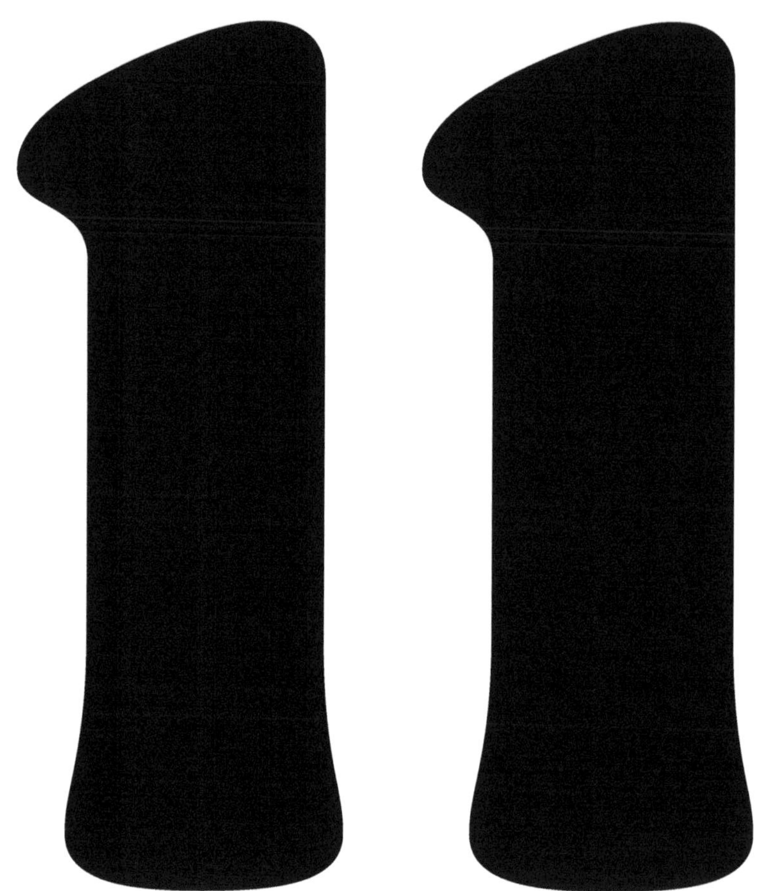

chapter eleven: standing alone

"Live the rest of your earthly life no longer concerned with human desires but consumed with what brings pleasure to God."

1 PETER 4:2

Sitting next to my computer is a picture of Heath from when he was about four years old. He's standing alone holding a single yellow flower, gazing at it as if it were the most beautiful flower he had ever seen. As I wrote this chapter and looked at the picture, God was reminding me how much beauty is found in standing alone. Over the last year, I have seen in scripture multiple times where God says that He desires for us to stand out and to look different from the world. I have always had a narrow mindset of what this looked like in one's life, and it wasn't until recently when I began to see that standing out requires a much deeper understanding of the convictions God has put in us. We aren't able to be obedient and walk this out without understanding our personal convictions and the deeper meaning of why they are there.

All four of our children are athletes and would spend every day of their lives on a court or a field if they could. Like Brandon, they are all competitive and all they want to do is play ball. It's funny because never in a million years did I imagine that this is what our life would look like because it is nothing like mine was growing up. I never really played sports because I really wasn't good at athletic things. I did a sport here and there, but nothing ever lasted long. Sports never took center stage in my life, so I was never faced with having to choose between God and sports. Of course I faced my own idols, as most teens do, but there wasn't a big thing in the equation that I had to constantly address. Sports has been the area where God has called our family to stand out and it hasn't been the easiest to choose obedience. It didn't take long for us to see that if all four of our kids did club sports then we would rarely attend church.

Heath's baseball team played in a tournament this past weekend that had a Sunday game at 9:30 in the morning. Even though Brandon and I knew where we stood on missing church, I won't lie and say that telling the coach that his first baseman wouldn't be there was an easy thing to do. After about an hour of talking, I asked Brandon to pray about it and just make the call because it made my stomach hurt too much to do it. We had recently told Brylee that she couldn't join a club volleyball team that played on Sunday mornings, so in my head this baseball decision was easy, but actually walking it out felt hard.

This is where my flesh began to play a role. My spirit felt strongly that Heath should be at church, yet my flesh was screaming even louder. What if the coach kicked him off the team? What if the coach started to play him less or hold it against our family? What if the team felt we had let them down and didn't like us anymore? I could go on and on with all the things my flesh was screaming, but you get it. I was worried about things that I couldn't control and things that had no eternal impact. At that moment, I wanted to just go with the flow. I mean, it was only one Sunday, but it wasn't about that one Sunday. I kept telling Brandon that I felt like it was a test. Looking back, that's exactly what it was. I had to finally ask myself if I was going to live out my convictions and choose an audience of one, or was I going to make things easy for everyone else while sacrificing what I felt in my heart? Going with the flow is easier in the moment, but the aftermath of the disobedience is hard no matter which conviction you are facing. Brandon chose for Heath to be at church, as I felt he would, but both of us had to choose to not worry what anyone else would think of our decision. We stood alone as a family, but we were secure in our decision to have an audience of one.

Going with the flow is easier in the moment, but the aftermath of the disobedience is hard no matter which conviction you are facing.

I used to watch families try to navigate tournaments and Sunday morning church, long before I was ever faced with it. Nearly every sports family I know plays in tournaments on Sunday mornings, and I don't judge or fault them for that. In all honesty, I used to because I didn't understand, but that is no longer my heart. When I was struggling to not have a judgmental heart, God reminded me of one of the first interactions I had with my friend, Kama. She brought up the topic of alcohol and how she doesn't ever allow herself to even take one sip. Before I could let myself wonder if she would judge me for having a drink, she said, "Just because this is my conviction doesn't mean that it's yours." At the time, I moved on pretty quickly and didn't really think much about it, but recently I have been reminding myself of the words she said "this is my conviction." I was able to respect her conviction even though I didn't share every part of it, and I was able to see how God convicts all of our hearts in different ways.

I do think there are many areas where God convicts us in similar ways, especially if we have the Holy Spirit living in us. The Ten Commandments would be a good example of where Christians usually all agree on similar guidelines. Unfortunately, there are other decisions that are not written out crystal clear in the Bible for us to follow. All we can do is lean into the Holy Spirit when we feel that pull. I would be tickled to death if the Bible told us how to handle Sunday sports tournaments, when to give our children a phone, what social media apps are best for each age, or what the healthiest age is to allow them to date. These are the big questions that many of us are facing and we don't want to get it wrong. I don't think there is a right or perfect answer that encompasses every family. I think there are general, healthy boundaries that we can set to protect their hearts, but when it's all said and done, each family has to make the call for their home. I wish I could say that every call I have made has been right for us, but that's not the case. I have had to learn, I have had to "take it back" after saying yes, and I have seen that all my children are different, which can sometimes mean that the boundary is different. Convictions are personal, which is why mine are unique from yours and vice versa.

Standing out will cost us, it will challenge us, and it will change us. Many want to stand out, but very few will be able to take that step because taking that step will always mean fighting our flesh harder than ever. There are many chapters in this book where it is hard to

Standing out will cost us, it will challenge us, and it will change us.

seek an audience of one, but for me this is one of the hardest areas because there are times when standing out means standing alone. I don't like to be alone or to feel different, but God continues to show me there is beauty in standing alone. Sometimes, He takes one small conviction and reveals so much of His heart through the decision-making process. The conversations, the tears, and understanding the why is so valuable to our faith. Seeing Heath's little tears when Brandon told him he would have to miss the game during church killed me, but knowing that Heath saw his Daddy do what was best for our family was priceless.

Can you see why standing out is complicated and shouldn't be compared? It's hard enough for each of us to figure out our own situations, which is why it's unnecessary and inappropriate to look at others and question their decisions. It's not our business, but man, what a hard thing that is to walk out at times. Most of us have a fleshly pull against standing out because of the criticism and repercussions we may face along the way. Just like in any situation, it is much easier to go with the flow and blend in because blending in doesn't cost us anything. Teens, I encourage you today to ask yourself how God is calling you to stand out in your life right now. Moms, I urge you to listen to the Holy Spirit and be obedient in this area because your kids are counting on you to protect them. It's easy to make decisions when our goal is to make others happy, but God desires for us to make decisions that align with how the Holy Spirit is leading us. Standing alone may be difficult, but choosing an audience of one when it comes to our decision making is priceless.

PROCESS AND REFLECT:

- Has God asked you to stand alone or go against what everyone else is doing? If so, write it out and maybe ask Him if there are any other areas where He wants you to look different from the rest of the world.

12

chapter twelve: protect your people

"Above all else, guard your heart, for everything you do flows from it."

PROVERBS 4:23

When I think of the word protect, I can't help but think back to a few years ago when the six of us were eating lunch at a Cheddar's before heading to the airport. It started off like any other meal with lots of conversations going on at once. All of the sudden, we heard very loud shouting from across the restaurant. Within seconds, a huge fight broke out between two family members sitting at the same table. I immediately told the kids to hide under the table and not to move. I knew I had to protect my children, and in that moment I would have done anything to keep them safe. Despite the circumstances, I was able to think calmly in the situation and get them out safely. At first, we waited under the table, but once I heard dishes breaking and saw things escalating, I told the kids to slowly follow me. I feared that someone would pull out a gun, so I started crawling towards the front door with the kids behind me. Looking back, I know that I did everything I could to get us out safely, but sometimes that is hard to do when you're in the midst of hard situations.

To protect means to shield, to guard, or to cover. There are times where we need to physically protect people, like that day at Cheddar's. There are also times it's important for us to emotionally protect our people. Too often, many fail to do this, which is why so many relationships end up broken or damaged. Once our emotions get to a certain point, it can feel impossible to repair the relationship. These broken relationships can typically lead to betrayal or abandonment. Walking away starts to feel easier and we allow ourselves to justify our separation in our minds. We see this often in marriage, but I want to focus on friendship for this chapter.

Over the last 43 years, I have walked many roads with different friendships. I have failed, I have succeeded, I have learned, and I have grown through each and every experience. Real friendships take honesty, they take intentionality, and they need to be protected. If we don't understand what protecting our people truly means, there will come a day where regret will be the lingering emotion that we can't seem to escape. How do I know this? Because, I have learned it the hard way. God has had me on this journey for a while, and I must say that learning to be a faithful friend hasn't come easily. What's funny is that I always thought I was a good friend, and I am not saying that I wasn't, but I realized there were so many times where I thought I was protecting my friend when I was actually slowly building walls. Walls that would eventually be difficult to tear down. The truth is that when we fail to protect what is valuable to us, we lose the people that are most important to us.

The truth is that when we fail to protect what is valuable to us, we lose the people that are most important to us.

So, what does it mean to protect your people? I want to share two areas with you where God has taught me how to seek an audience of one, even in my friendships.

1. PROTECT THE INTEGRITY OF THE FRIENDSHIP

Integrity is the quality of being honest. Honest with your feelings, honest with your hurts, and honest when it's hard to be honest. Integrity is also the state of being whole and undivided. Choosing to protect the integrity of your friendship can only be done through honesty because dishonesty will divide even without ever saying a word.

One of the hardest things I had to realize is that sometimes protecting our people means confronting our people. I know, I know, this is not what anyone wants to hear. Confrontation and conflict are two words that send most people the other direction. Just the thought of these things is enough to bring on an anxiety attack! I get it. There is nothing fun about having a hard conversation, but there is also nothing fun about holding things in for years or feeling like parts of your friendship are a lie. Either way you choose to do it, life has a way of flipping over all the cards that you're trying to avoid being shown. The difference is that having the hard talk on your terms allows you to prayerfully go into it with the desire to protect the friendship instead of going into it with the desire to protect only yourself. Once we get to the place where we are angry and have had enough, we tend to enter the conversation defensively and our only desire is for our side to be seen or heard. Somewhere along the way, we lose the desire to see where the other person is coming from. That is when it becomes extremely difficult for the friendship to come out ahead.

I think many fall into the trap thinking that confronting someone with anything but roses will lead to worse conflict, but what I am saying is that avoiding biblical advice causes many of us to wind up in broken situations. For years I have been taught to speak truth in love, regardless of how intimidating it can be. These "truth and love" moments are crucial in a friendship, especially one that you view as intimate or close. When we allow someone we love to act in a way that does not honor God, we are enabling them. We are not responsible for other people's actions, but we are responsible for our own. Choosing to not take the hard step allows the Enemy to begin to work in our thoughts, which is the exact moment the pieces start to fall apart. Yes, it's scary to sit down with someone you love and say something hard. There is no doubt about that, but avoiding it only postpones the hard conversation and usually turns it into something even harder. This often leads to poor choice of words and reactions once it is addressed. My fear of a friend's potential reaction has trumped what I knew was right in my heart many times. However, protecting someone you love means wanting the very best for them even if it means sacrificing feeling good while you're doing it.

I am thankful to have friends that keep me accountable. Accountability has not only kept me grounded during rocky times, but it has been the thing to bring me back when I got off track. Without my friends' accountability, I know I would have continued down a path to complete destruction. We have all heard of the slow fade and how making life-changing decisions doesn't happen overnight. These life-changing decisions start with compromising small parts of ourselves a little at a time. Before we know it, we find ourselves in trouble. Godly friendships should play a role by stepping in before things get out of hand. Godly friendships should see the red flags that ultimately motivate us to go to our friend in love. Godly friendships are more than just fun lunches where everyone masks the things that are really happening inside of their lives and hearts. I tell my girls over and over that Godly friendships start with being a Godly friend. Godly friends are honest, they walk in integrity, and they do hard things when the Holy Spirit leads.

I tell my girls over and over that Godly friendships start with being a Godly friend.

There is a time for keeping quiet and there is a time for being bold. Only the Holy Spirit can show you when to open this door. Trust me, I have chosen God's way enough times for me to see that it can be done well and you can be stronger on the other side if you follow where the Holy Spirit leads you. When our audience is God, we will be obedient to follow through in hard situations, regardless of the "what ifs" we are rehearsing in our mind.

2. PROTECT THEIR STORY

Years ago, I remember my friend, Kerri, saying something to me that really impacted my thinking. I had been going through a very hard time in my life and opened up to her about many of the private battles I was fighting through. Anytime you let someone in, like really in, it's a risk. I knew this, but I also felt peace about trusting her with my story. I remember one day we were sitting by the pool and I jokingly told her she was stuck with me because she knew too much about me. Yes, I was partly joking, but there was another part of me that felt fearful knowing that another person knew very intimate details about my life. I will never forget her response to me that day. She said, "I will never share your story with anyone. Even if I move far away or we have a falling out and aren't friends anymore, it would never be my place to share your story." From that day on, I never doubted her loyalty to me or her respect for what I had walked through. I had always been someone that people could confide in, but what Kerri said that day echoed to me that there is never a reason to share someone else's story. No matter what.

Protecting someone means choosing to honor them by the way you speak to them and the way you speak about them.

Protecting someone's story goes beyond not sharing their personal information. Protecting their story means never choosing to use their past or their experiences against them to prove a point. It means defending them when they are not in the room and can't defend themselves. Protecting someone means choosing to honor them by the way you speak to them and the way you speak about them. I tell my girls all the time that there will come a day when you have to choose whether or not you are going to choose integrity or comfort. Choosing comfort will feel easier in the moment, but choosing integrity will feel good forever.

I recently heard a few words that have been on repeat in my mind: "We can only take our kids as far as we have come." We can't teach them how to behave in ways that we don't behave.

Choosing comfort will feel easier in the moment, but choosing integrity will feel good forever.

We can't help them overcome issues that still have us in bondage. We can't show them how to be a faithful friend if we don't model it for them. This is the reason I want to keep growing and continue doing better in every single area. Their friendships will make or break so many parts of their lives, so why not teach them how to do it well from the beginning?

One last thing, faithful friends cannot be replaced even when new friendships enter our lives. I have been blessed with friends that have been a true gift to me throughout many different seasons of my life. Years ago, one of my daughters asked me, "Mommy, who is your best friend?" I giggled, knowing that there was no way I could ever choose because each friend held a special place in my heart. My high school friends have my heart because we grew up together, we anticipated our first kisses together, and we learned how to be a person together. Never in a million years could they be replaced with another soul. I have friends from when I was a newlywed, ones I raised babies with, and ones I learned how to be a mom with.

I have friends who sat with me when I hit rock bottom and had nothing left to give. They fought for me in prayer, they took care of my kids when I was too weak to do so, and they carried me through some of the hardest times of my life. They did all of this while protecting me and my heart along the way. At the age of 44, I have friends in my life right now who I am raising teenage girls with. God knew I needed these friends and knew they would need to be grounded in the Word of God. It's so hard to be a mom during this season and to know what step to take or not to take next. My friends who are walking by my side don't simply give me their advice; they lead me to the Word and pray for my kids with me. Every single one of these friends are irreplaceable and extremely valuable to me. Being a faithful friend means understanding every part of what it looks like to be a healthy friend, so that we can love and support each other well without allowing jealousy or insecurity to get in the way.

I recently spoke to a group of women about friendship, and I used the word friendship to share qualities I felt were important in being a good friend. If you're looking for a good friend, or even if you have many friends, these pieces are critical in building lifelong friendships that can withstand all the things life brings our way!

F: Flesh must die. Our flesh can come out in ways like selfishness, jealousy or even comparison. If we are not careful, our flesh has a way of damaging our people.. Pray for self-control so you don't walk in the flesh!

R: Real over fake. Remember, it's possible to be fully known AND fully loved. If we are seeking deep friendships then we must be honest.

I: Intentionality. Don't wait for the invite every time! Seek out your people and make them feel loved and special. Be the one who sends the texts and lets someone know you're thinking of them. If we are not intentional then it becomes so easy for our friendships to drift.

E. Earnestly value one another. God made each person and friend different for a reason. Too often, we want others to be like us, respond like us, and operate like us. When we try to change people, whether it be a friend or a spouse, oftentimes it causes hurt and division. Look at each person as unique and allow God to use them in your life.

N. Necessary boundaries. Our friends are not meant to meet all of our needs. Once we realize that, we will automatically have healthier friendships. We all know the friendships that suck us dry, and after a while, all we want is distance from those friends. It's so important to not have unrealistic expectations of our friends because that will only lead to disappointment.

D. Desire accountability. If we want to live in community with others, then we must realize that community should come with accountability. If a friend comes to mein love, I should be humbled and willing to hear her heart. Getting defensive isn't good for anyone. I want friends that make me better. I want to be the kind of friend that pulls others up! This takes accountability even when it's tough.

S. Seek the Holy Spirit. Seek Him first. Seek the Holy Spirit before you make a phone call to handle a conflict. Seek Him before you respond or react so that your words are honoring. Seek Him and thank the Lord when things are good and let Him be your first prayer when things get hard. This will change everything.

H. Have a humble heart. Pride pushes people away, humility draws them in. Let's stop the show and admit that life can be very challenging. The sooner we walk in humility, the sooner God can strengthen connections that will draw us closer to Him.

I. Integrity over loyalty. I learned this the hard way but I learned the lesson well. What is right has to trump the loyalty we feel for another person. I have learned that I can't have someone's back, no matter who they are, if their actions are not aligning with scripture. This is a tough one, especially for friendships we've had for a long time, but having integrity has to win in the end.

P. Pursue Jesus together. It sounds so simple, but this is the glue that will hold your friendship together. When we share the same goal and pursue the same God, there is power working within the friendship. I have seen it and I believe it. When I pray for the friends I am struggling with, it's so much harder to be angry at them. Being on the same page, especially spiritually, will allow the friendship to go deeper and be able to push through so much more.

Striving to walk through friendship with an audience of one is crucial for success. When our audience is our friends, and making them happy, then more than likely things won't end well for that friendship somewhere down the road. The reason for this is the simple fact that we usually fail to be obedient to the spirit when our goal is to make another person happy.

Sometimes the Holy Spirit pushes us to do hard things, and it's much easier to be obedient when our audience is God alone. Think of it like this, if you truly want to be a good friend then fix your eyes on the Lord and align your thoughts and heart with His. When we do this, our friends will see Jesus in us and they will trust our motives because they will be pure and unselfish. Decide now that you are going to be the person who goes above and beyond to protect your people. I encourage you to guard the integrity of the friendship with everything in you and to hold every story near and dear to your heart in the same way you'd want someone else to do for you.

PROCESS AND REFLECT:

- Take a few minutes to write down the names of a few friends and evaluate these friendships. Write down the areas you're doing well in each friendship, as well as the areas where there is room for growth.
- Ask yourself one last thing; "Are my closest friends drawing me towards Jesus or pulling me away?" Sometimes it's important for our friendships to shift if we get to the place where they are not honoring the Lord. If there is one thing I want my girls to remember, it's this; **The people you choose to share your life with will have a huge impact on your future!** So choose wisely!

13

chapter thirteen: grit

"Whatever you do, work at it with all your heart, as working for the Lord, not for human masters."

COLOSSIANS 3:23

Grit is not a word that seems to be used often, but it is a word that has been the driving force in my life for many years. To me, grit is another way of describing the passion and perseverance that lives within a person. Everyone has a different level of grit and all of us demonstrate that level in our own way. There have been times in my life when my mom might say that I had too much grit because I lacked the ability to stop pushing myself in moments where I put my health at risk in order to achieve the goal. This is a story of one of those times.

At the age of 23, I set out with the goal to run a half marathon. I had never been a runner until I met my college roommate, Robyn. One mile at a time, she turned me into someone that actually enjoyed the sport. There was something I loved about getting up early when everyone else was still asleep and hitting the pavement. Over time, it became therapeutic for me, so I continued running even after we graduated and moved apart. During that first year of working in the real world, Robyn and I decided that we would train for the race separately and meet in Nashville to run the race together. I worked so hard preparing for the race. I was determined to show up to the race, stronger than ever, and nothing was going to stop me from crossing that finish line!

During my training, I endured a knee injury. I continued to train, all while downing bottles of Aleve to try to numb the pain so that nothing would stand in the way of the race. I remember the medicine helping get me through the runs, but I had no idea what it was doing to me on the inside. The morning of the race, I felt so good and so ready! I knew that I had given everything I had in training, and I couldn't wait to cross the finish line. However, I found myself sicker than ever at mile three of the race. I had no idea what was wrong, but I knew something wasn't right. The pain in my stomach was so severe, but my heart knew that I had to finish the race. The pain in my stomach made the last 10 miles memorable, but not in a positive way.

Somewhere along the race, I made the decision that I wasn't going to quit regardless of how bad it got, and it got really bad. To make a long story short, I finished the race and then found myself on the bathroom floor throwing up blood. As you can imagine, that landed me in a hospital bed. It's been over 20 years since that day, but I still remember it like it was yesterday. I even remember the doctor coming into my room and telling me my race time right before he told me that I ran the whole thing with a bleeding ulcer in my stomach. It was epic—or maybe idiotic. Either way, it became the moment when I realized that I could do anything I set my heart to do. Before that day, I am not sure that I really believed in myself or believed that I could do hard things. Crossing that finish line while enduring such great pain was me proving to myself that I had unstoppable grit that could persevere through anything.

Sometimes in our lives we face pivotal moments that shape us in such a way that we are changed forever.

Looking back and knowing what I know now, I wish I could say that I should have stopped running that day, but that's not the case. (Sorry, Mom!) Sometimes in our lives we face pivotal moments that shape us in such a way that we are changed forever. Finishing that race was that moment for me. Being able to dig deep and hold tight to that grit is oftentimes the difference between finishing strong or quitting when the road gets hard. Since that race, I have faced many "bleeding ulcer moments" where it would have been much easier to quit than endure the pain of walking through the situation. I knew what deep pain felt like, but I also knew what hanging on and finishing well felt like.

Grit is necessary on this journey because it's not easy seeking an audience of one. The road gets long, and doing the hard work to seek Him first can be tiresome. Learning to seek an audience of one is a daily choice. Sometimes, it's an hourly choice, and it's not for the faint of heart. Many people will try, but very few will feel successful because they have never had to access the grit required to make it happen. I am here to tell you that you can do anything you put your heart to if you have the power of Jesus behind you! We are capable of so much more than we give ourselves credit for, and when you put the redemptive power of Jesus in the mix anything is possible. There was a time in my life when I wasn't sure if I believed the verse that says, "Nothing is impossible with God." But I will tell you this, as a 43-year-old woman standing here today, I believe that verse with all my heart.

Instead, I urge you to start running towards the redemptive healing that your heart longs for.

I don't believe that we can just sit back and expect God to do it all, though. There will come a day in all of our lives where we will find ourselves in an impossible situation. Maybe you are there right now in an impossible marriage, a strangling addiction, a past that continues to haunt your present, a hopeless friendship, or a prayer you've been praying so long that you don't believe it will ever be answered. I have faced all of the above and have gotten to the other side, but that's only because I chose to keep running. I chose to put one foot in front of the other, I chose to cling to Jesus through the pain, and I chose to do whatever it took to find freedom in each and every situation. I ran THROUGH the bleeding ulcer! I didn't lay on the couch with a victim mentality and expect Jesus to do the work for me. Sure, there were moments where I felt sorry for myself, but at some point you must get up and run the race yourself. It's time to stop allowing anyone else to write your story. Instead, I urge you to start running towards the redemptive healing that your heart longs for. Regardless of the situation, I promise you that it will be a race worth running and one that will bring heart-changing moments that will build your faith like never before.

PROCESS AND REFLECT:

- What in your life do you want to quit right now because it feels too hard or impossible?
- Do you see benefits to sticking it out if you were able to fight through it? What are they?
- If you feel there are biblical reasons or wisdom that are weighing on you to quit, list those too! Sometimes God does want us to walk away from situations or relationships that are toxic.

14

chapter fourteen: exposed

"For there is nothing hidden that will not be exposed, and nothing concealed that will not be known or brought out into the open."

LUKE 8:17

Exposed. Whew, this has always felt like such a loaded word to me. Exposed simply means visible or no longer hidden. No matter what the context of the situation, being exposed is oftentimes the moment where we find ourselves in a very vulnerable position. The emotions that cloud our minds once we are exposed are embarrassment, defensiveness, fear, shame, discomfort, or even anxiety. Eve was the first woman to be exposed. Her initial response was shame, and her immediate action was to hide. I think back to moments where I felt completely exposed. It's not exactly the best feeling in the world. Whether you're laying naked in a gown for a yearly check-up at the OB or caught in a web of lies that has been brought to light, it seems like the feelings we face can be similar. There's no doubt that it's very uncomfortable to have something about you or your life exposed, but I also believe that there are things that need to be brought into the light if we are seeking healing or deliverance from them.

Years ago, I was lifting weights with my trainer. We were just talking away as I did my squats. All of the sudden, I felt a horrible pain in my booty and freaked out. Yes, my booty! I knew something was really wrong, but I managed to get through the rest of the workout without making it a big deal. Over the next few days, Google was my best friend as I tried to figure out what might have happened to cause the pain in my booty. I knew I needed to get help, but I was so nervous to go see a doctor. At first, I thought maybe it was a hemorrhoid because of the situation that caused it, but the more I read and the more painful it got, I knew it had to be more than that. It took me about a week to finally call the doctor to make an appointment. I knew that going to see a butt doctor was going to be super awkward and I had to work my way up to it. In all honesty, I also had to get to the point where I couldn't live with the pain anymore. It's like I waited until it was unbearable before I decided that getting help would be worth the embarrassment of the appointment.

I will never forget that appointment because at that moment I felt extremely exposed. I started off with a female doctor, but once she realized she needed help, she had to call in the 30-year-old guy that also worked in the office. That was fantastic, as you can only imagine. Most things don't embarrass me, but when she opened the door to the hallway and yelled, "I need someone to come hold butt cheeks," I literally thought I was going to fall over and die. For those who worked in the office, it was a normal request. I mean, she's a butt doctor! But for me, I felt more exposed than ever. The next few minutes were a blur because I was trying to breathe slowly so I didn't pass out from the extreme mental and physical discomfort. Turns out, I had a huge blood clot that had to be cut before I would have any relief from that throbbing pain. She gave me a choice. I could wait it out or let her handle it right there. I told her to handle it. As awful as those moments were, I knew I didn't want to go another minute dealing with pain that could be eliminated.

I sat here for a while today debating whether or not to put this story in here. It's a little much and crosses a few privacy boundaries for me, but God used it to teach me some life-changing thought patterns so I decided to go for it. I am sure I am not the only one who has experienced awkward moments that you wish you could forget, right?

I lived a long time without ever understanding the beauty of living in the light.

I lived a long time without ever understanding the beauty of living in the light. It seems like most of us live with the mindset that says we are entitled to our private lives and don't owe anyone an explanation. Our pride rehearses thoughts that say we can think what we want, we can do what we want, and no one needs to worry about us. It's easy to get caught up in this mindset, but we have to be careful because too much of this leads to a life that lacks accountability. I know it never turns out well for me when I do what I want and stiff-arm accountability. Scripture tells us the importance of living life with others and walking in the light, but I feel like social media has allowed us to only shine a light on the good things in our lives.

I have never met a person who wants to share all of the bad things that have happened to them with the whole world, but constantly sharing only our good moments has left many feeling inadequate, isolated, and alone in their struggles. Because of this, I feel like many are walking through life in the dark. I tell my kids over and over that the Enemy loves to work in the dark. When we hide and keep secrets, the Enemy is able to have his way with our thoughts day after day. Not disclosing our thoughts leads to actions and behaviors that could have been avoided. Everything starts in our minds! When we bring hard things into the light, the Enemy can be defeated and God can set us free before things unravel and get out of hand.

The older I get, the more I can say that I want to be fully exposed when it comes to my thoughts and my actions. I have seen what secrets can do to a person and the path it takes them down. I don't want any part of that. I have been there and done that, which is why I want everything exposed every single day. The depression battle that I shared early on in this book started with hiding, a prideful heart, and fearful thoughts of what others would think if they knew every part of my story. The Enemy had me so trapped by these fears that I found myself laying on that closet floor not wanting to face another day. Darkness is a powerful thing, especially when we are facing it alone. I still tell my friends that I could never truly get them to see how bad off I was because you can't explain the depth of darkness with words. Darkness overwhelms our spirit in such a way that we actually believe the lies the Enemy is shooting our way. It's such a dangerous place to find yourself in and an even more dangerous place to stay in.

Ask yourself right now, what areas are you living in the dark? In what ways are your

Darkness is a powerful thing, especially when we are facing it alone.

thoughts and actions sitting in darkness? You may say that you are not currently struggling with big things or big sins, but even something like jealousy can brew into many sinful actions when it's kept in the dark. Heck, many of the stories in the Old Testament where big sins occurred were originally rooted in jealousy. When we don't address what is in the dark, we tend to find ourselves in situations where we are capable of falling into any temptation known to man. You and I are not exempt from the big stuff, especially when we fail to address the root issues in our hearts and minds.

I guess you could say it took battling my demons in the dark for me to fully grasp the freedom that is found when we surrender our secrets into the hands of Jesus. Whether you are in a tug-a-war with an unhealthy thought or you're knee-deep in sexual sin, I have found that the only way to find freedom is to shed some light through the darkness. I tried every other way for years, failing over and over until the moment I exposed my sins. That was the moment God said, "Okay, you're ready to face this and you're ready for me to restore you." It's almost like taking that step of humility was the hardest step, but once I did, I could breathe again and knew that I was going to be okay.

There will come a day when the pain is so great that it is not worth holding it in any longer.

Remember how I told you that it took me experiencing the absolute worst booty pain in order for me to humble myself to walk into that office? It's no different with emotional pain, alcohol addictions, depression, porn addictions, eating disorders, jealousy, insecurities, affairs…I could go on and on forever. There will come a day when the pain is so great that it is not worth holding it in any longer. Will it be hard to bring it into the light? Absolutely. Will it be awkward, painful, and embarrassing at times? Probably so. Are you going to have to do the hard work and pick up the pieces from living in the darkness? Yes, you are. But I'll tell you one thing, after the doctor addressed my issue I was able to walk out the door without excruciating pain. Sure, I still had a lot of healing to do, but I could walk out feeling relieved, knowing that I was headed in the right direction. Living in the darkness will never bring relief and that, my friends, will lead to hopelessness. I don't want anyone reading this to continue living like that.

There has to come a day when you realize your freedom is more important than what others might think of you.

I will leave you with this thought. Bringing something into the light doesn't mean you have to tell the whole world or post it on social media. For many, it means finding one trusted person to help you walk through the hard thing and keep you accountable. As I left the doctor that day, I giggled and told her it takes a special person to do her job and I was thankful that she could handle my situation. Ask God to show you who that person is for you. Not everyone can handle every part of your story or provide you guidance to support your healing. I encourage you to ask the Lord, and seek Him first in your decisions, because I believe He will bring clarity as to who those friends should be. I promise you one thing, there is so much beauty in living a life that is exposed versus a life lived in hiding. We have to remember that God sees all of us, so when we hide, it's simply us living for an audience of many instead of an audience of one. There has to come a day when you realize your freedom is more important than what others might think of you. Living in the light is the way to get there!

PROCESS AND REFLECT:

- This is a tough one, but what are you hiding in your life? Are they thoughts that only you know about? Are they actions you feel guilty about? Remember, the Enemy loves to work in the dark, especially in the things we keep secret.

15

chapter fifteen: drunk

"Do not get drunk on wine, which leads to debauchery. Instead, be filled with the spirit."

EPHESIANS 5:18

I think most of us could say that there was a time in our life where we were drawn to the idea of being drunk. I think what drew me in before I had ever had a sip of alcohol was the curiosity that is always attached to the unknown. Curiosity has a way of tempting all of us because it stirs up an urge to want to know more about something or how something might feel. We could all fill in the blanks of something that has consumed our minds simply because of the curiosity of it. I am currently seeing this curiosity unfold right before me while raising girls and hearing them talk about having their first kiss. Brylee is 15 years old and would say that she's not quite ready to take that step. However, there are also days when she says, "I just want to go for it so that I know what it's like and to get it over with!" Curiosity is sometimes the thing that convinces our hearts to say yes even if we know it may land us in a compromising situation. Curiosity is a powerful desire that we all need to be extremely aware of so that we can make choices using wisdom instead of whatever feeling we might be having that day.

I remember one of the first times I got drunk. I'm shaking my head after writing that sentence, because usually you don't remember being drunk. Let me rephrase, I remember the aftermath of one of the first times my curiosity got the best of me and I drank way too much. I lived a sheltered life growing up. My closest friends were from my youth group. We spent our weekends at church events and in sleeping bags having girl talks. I never really thought about going out on the weekends or being a party girl. High school was very calm when it came to partying, but there's no doubt that I changed things up in college.

My first year of college was wild in every way possible. I went to The University of Texas at Arlington. I was living on my own for the first time and trying to keep a job so that I could pay rent. My friend Lauren and I didn't really know anyone, so we joined a sorority, which was probably my first step down the dark path. I had been surrounded by my family and my Jesus friends my whole life, so diving into an extremely worldly environment that first year of college was a culture shock, for a girl like me. As different as it was, it didn't take long for my behaviors to start looking like the rest of the world. Scripture says that we can't flirt with the world's ways or else we'll start to look like the world, which is exactly what happened to me. I spent my nights drinking and staying up way too late so often that skipping class became a normal thing. Before I knew it, I had lost all self-discipline and the only motivation I had was to make enough money so that I could afford the new life that I had created.

Scripture says that we can't flirt with the world's ways or else we'll start to look like the world, which is exactly what happened to me.

Looking back, I often wonder how I lasted almost a year in the midst of that lifestyle. I remember there being times when I would look in the mirror and feel so much anger at the way I was behaving, but for months I continued down a path that I knew didn't lead to anywhere good. I was stuck in this cycle of drinking alcohol to escape my feelings and waking up the next morning to those feelings resurfacing because the alcohol only took them away temporarily. The definition of drunk that stands out most to me is this; "finding yourself in a place where you have lost control over your physical and/or mental functions." I like this definition because it has really opened my eyes to the fact that a person can be drunk on things other than alcohol. Any time we use something to alter our mind, it can lead to drunkenness.

When I think about those first few times I drank too much, I remember having foggy thoughts of the night before and numerous negative emotions when I woke up the next morning, along with feeling very sick and confused. I struggled to remember things the next day. I always felt so insecure because I worried if I acted like an idiot in front of others. I see now that these are very real responses when we choose to swallow a pill or drink a drink that is meant to change the way that we think and feel. The sole purpose of these things is to help a person relax their mind, but when they're used in excess they change the entire behavior of the person. When I am not in control of my own emotions or actions, I get fearful. That fear always leads to insecurity. It's important to see that many teens and adults will use substances to feel more secure, but the end result usually leads to a deeper insecurity. The problem is the deeper we fall into insecurity, the more substances or addictions we run to in order to numb that pain. Therefore, an activity that started out as just a curiosity is now the thing causing your life to crumble right before your eyes.

I pulled myself together after that first year and was able to transfer to a smaller school with more accountability. It was a life-changing move for me. I spent years trying to fight the temptation to go back to those old habits. I am not going to lie, those habits felt good at the time because I had so much pain inside of my heart and didn't know how to deal with any of it. I was overweight, which caused many insecurities and spiraling thoughts daily. I carried so much shame because I had been raised to know better, yet I failed miserably the minute I was set free to live on my own. I was always uncomfortable smiling or talking because I didn't have a pretty smile, which was something I had carried since that boy in 7th grade told me that my smile was ugly. My GPA was low from all of the classes I skipped, so I had a heavy school load to try to recover from that. I was carrying a lot and didn't know any other way to escape the burdens. I fought hard and surrounded myself with people who would encourage healthy habits, but it wasn't until later on in my life when God would show me another way.

The Bible talks about being "drunk in the Spirit." It sounds kind of odd when you think about being drunk and the Holy Spirit in the same sentence, but I can assure you it's a real thing. It's actually a really amazing thing that has changed my life. I have talked to so many teen girls and women who all say they desire to truly feel the Holy Spirit. These women have been Christians for years, but their heart has never been overwhelmed with the Holy Spirit. I believe this is why so many of us are seeking out things like alcohol, drugs, sex, pornography, and social media. We are searching for something to give us those feelings because we don't understand how to seek the power of God that He has to offer us.

Regardless of our ages, the heart of a woman beats with many of the same desires.

All of us want to feel something inside. All of us want to experience moments where our brain stops worrying about life and can simply rest. All of us desire peace in the midst of an immensely broken world. We are all the same when it comes to this! Regardless of our ages, the heart of a woman beats with many of the same desires. It's gut-wrenching to watch women search for peace in the wrong places. It's terrifying to watch our children search for security in substances or other people. It's so easy to see others searching for something more in others, but many of us are walking around doing the same thing. We want to be drunk on something so that we don't have to feel anything!

Ephesians 5:18 tells us to not be drunk on wine but to be filled with the Holy Spirit. This statement is so simple and so clear. When I read this verse, I believe that they are coupled together because God knows the desires of our hearts, both good and bad. He knows that we will desire the wrong things if we don't know what it feels like to be filled with the Holy Spirit. It is so important that Christians understand this because Christianity is usually not what brings people to Jesus. People are drawn to Jesus through the Holy Spirit and through moments where the Holy Spirit is moving. In Acts, over 3,000 people came to know Jesus because the Holy Spirit was moving through Peter as he preached. The ones that were filled

People are drawn to Jesus through the Holy Spirit and through moments where the Holy Spirit is moving.

with the Spirit were accused of being drunk on new wine, but they were actually drunk in the Holy Spirit! When the Holy Spirit moves, minds are altered and hearts are changed.

I vividly remember standing in a Chris Tomlin worship concert once and saying to myself, "This feeling is better than being drunk or anything I have ever felt before!" It was the truth! To be drunk in the Spirit means that we will lose the ability to control our every thought because it's like God steps in to run the show. In the moments where I have felt the Spirit the most, I felt like I was in a different world. I didn't care who was around me or who was watching me worship. I felt God so strongly that my heart was beating only for Him and nothing else. I didn't have a care in the world, and you want to know the best part? When I woke up the next day, I felt so secure and so amazing from head to toe. When we experience the Holy Spirit, I believe we are purified in such a way that brings freedom and a new hope. There is no drug, pornographic site, or alcoholic beverage that can meet the desperate need we have to feel whole inside. The Holy Spirit is the only source capable of altering our minds in the sweetest way, leaving us feeling whole and secure on the other side of the experience.

Before I end this chapter, I want to share three tips I learned to pursue drunkenness in the spirit versus drunkenness from wine or worldly outlets.

1. CHOOSE TO LIVE YOUR LIFE WITH PEOPLE WHO HAVE QUALITIES THAT YOU DESIRE TO HAVE

I have seen girls and women distance themselves from others that intimidate them or do things better than them. Instead of leaning in and learning how to grow, they almost push them away or find reasons to put them down. It's a funny thing, but we end up losing when we choose to let our jealousy win in those moments. Not only are we not growing, but now we also have a heart filled with jealousy. When thinking of how my own friends have helped me grow, I can't help but think of my friend Melissa and her gift to truly celebrate people. The more I am around her, the more I grow in celebrating other people. Years ago when I was a runner, my friend Ashley and I would feed off of each other so much that we became faster than we ever thought possible. No, we weren't winning first place, but I had never ran so fast in my life. We made each other better because we came together instead of competing against one another. When I am around my friend Stasia, my heart immediately softens because of her spirit and her joy. She has helped me so many times without even knowing it. The people you hang around will ultimately rub off on you, whether that be good or bad, but if you want to learn how to walk in the Holy Spirit then you need to surround yourself with people who are living that out! Learning to walk in the Spirit instead of your flesh is a learning process. The more you see it in others, the more you will desire it, and the more opportunities you'll have for those special moments. Pick friends that make you want to be a better person and you can't go wrong!

2. SHOW UP TO THE PLACES THAT WILL SET YOU UP FOR SUCCESS!

You can't go to a church if you want to be drunk with wine, and you can't hang out in a bar when you want your heart to be filled with the Holy Spirit! It's simple! Signing up for retreats, camps, worship nights, Christian concerts, women's small groups, or a night out with other women who love Jesus are good ways to put yourself into situations that will lead to opportunities for spiritual growth. Sure, you're always going to find people in those settings that are not authentic, but you have to start somewhere. You know your struggles, your tendencies, and the things you need to stay away from so choose your activities wisely. It's no different than removing the cookies out of the pantry when you're having the kind of week that is going to end with you eating the whole package. Throw the cookies away before they are a problem! Teens, you may be able to handle hanging out at a party and not giving in to the temptation, but I promise you that there will come a time when you will fall. You are human!

3. PRAY AND ASK GOD TO SHOW UP AND REVEAL THE HOLY SPIRIT TO YOU

I love the lyrics in a song that says, "Holy Spirit you are welcome here!" Our hearts should be ready to invite Him in. As our hearts strive to walk in purity, eyes are opened. So many times we can't see or feel the Spirit because we are so distracted by our own sin and the mess around us. The Bible says, "Blessed are the pure at heart for they will see God." This verse is true and I have seen it play out in my own life. Yes, God has spoken to me in the midst of my mess, but the way He has spoken to and through me when I have walked in purity is a whole different story. We have to be ready, available and expectant for the presence of God to show up in our lives, so let's pursue Him and ask Him!

Yes, God has spoken to me in the midst of my mess, but the way He has spoken to and through me when I have walked in purity is a whole different story.

Trust me, when I say that being filled with the Spirit will rock your world much more than four shots of tequila on a Friday night will. We all desire to be drunk on something, but man, I encourage you to be drunk on the things that will fill your soul and lead you to freedom in Christ! There's no doubt in my mind that being filled with the Holy Spirit will end better for you.

PROCESS AND REFLECT:

- If you have ever been drunk, what part of it did you enjoy? Or did you not enjoy any of it? Think about what draws you to become intoxicated in any way.
- Have you ever felt The Holy Spirit move powerfully in your life? Describe that time and what it was like for you.

16

chapter sixteen: surrendered obedience

"For whosoever will save his life shall lose it; and whosoever will lose his life will save it for my sake."

MATTHEW 16:25

How many Google fans do I have out there? You know what I'm talking about, the ones that run to Google the minute they need help with anything. You see a small red spot on your arm and soon enough Google has you thinking that you're dying because you have read every possible cause for this little red spot. Maybe you're the type that believes everything that Google says, so you follow all the steps as if it were the best advice you have ever been given. If I am being honest, I have fallen into that category. Well, at least I used to before I learned my lesson the hard way.

Back in my 30s, I was leading those summer boot camps that I told you about. Texas summers are extremely hot, and by the end of the workouts we would be dripping in sweat. Every inch of my body was soaked, including my shorts. I had little kids at the time, so it would be hours before I had a chance to change or shower. Disgusting, I know, but I operated in survival mode during those years, and Mama came last.

If you have had any experience with UTIs or yeast infections, you know that sitting in wet swimsuits or clothes is the absolute worst situation ever. Sure enough, I found myself with a terrible yeast infection that summer. It was so bad that I cringe even while typing this out. The itching and burning were so severe that I would cover the bottom half of my body in ice packs just to try and escape the torture for a few minutes. Long story short, the over-the-counter medicine wasn't working. Even the prescription medicine I tried failed to work. Instead of following the doctor's advice, I thought it would be really smart to ask Google if it had any home remedies or suggestions for me. I am sure that you can imagine that this doesn't have a good ending. You're right. It doesn't, but let me play this out for you so you know how unwise it was to trust Google.

Google said to pour apple cider vinegar on your hoo-ha and let it sit. I didn't read much else after that because I used to be very quick to react and didn't think too much about the details. So there I was, lying in an awkward position in my bathroom, pouring apple cider vinegar all over the area. It took about two seconds before I was screaming at the top of my lungs because I literally thought I was going to die. Just imagine your hoo-ha burning like a fire that is blazing across a field. That's about what it felt like. All I remember was screaming, crying, and yelling at Brandon that he needed to take me to the ER. If you know Brandon, you know that he is extremely calm and always thinks before he does things. Naturally, his first words asked me why I would ever do something like this. It was not the time for that, which he realized pretty quickly, then he said, "What do you think the doctor is going to say when you tell him that you poured apple cider vinegar down there?"

I hadn't really thought that far or about the immense embarrassment I would feel waddling into that hospital. At that moment, I just wanted the pain to stop. The next few hours were a blur, but my calm husband had several ideas that kept me from having to make that dreadful trip to the ER. To this day, God uses this story to remind me of a few things. One, I am glad that I have a husband who is the opposite of me and can think logically in heated situations. Two, Google doesn't always give the best advice. Three, always read all of the directions. I went back later only to see that it said to put a few drops of the vinegar into the water before pouring it on (not pour it straight out of the bottle!). That felt wonderful to read after the fact. Four, why am I so quick to listen to Google but drag my feet when I feel the Lord telling me to do something? Ouch! That last one hurt and has continued to hurt over the last 10 years as God has retrained my brain to live with my hands open wide in complete obedience.

Obedience is something that has never been easy for anyone. We are all born into this world with a sinful flesh that seeks to fulfill our selfish needs and desires. It doesn't matter if it's a two-year-old wanting to get out of the highchair at a restaurant against their parent's wishes, the teenager who purposely hides apps on their phone against their parent's rules, or the woman crossing boundaries in her job or any other area in her life. We were born with a disobedient heart, and that is the bottom line! To be disobedient means to refuse to do what someone is asking you to do. I am sure every parent can agree that it doesn't feel good when you are dealing with a disobedient or rebellious child. Their age doesn't even matter. When a child refuses to do what you ask, it's almost like your body and mind freak out because it can be so bothersome.

I can't help but wonder how God feels when we refuse to do something that He is asking us to do.

I can't help but wonder how God feels when we refuse to do something that He is asking us to do. I know He is a loving God, but I am sure it's frustrating when He knows and sees the big picture of our lives, and we stay unwilling to obey Him. When it comes to our daily lives, obedience plays out in so many ways. When I look back on my own life, I can identify several times when it was hard to be obedient when I knew God was asking me to make a move. It reminds me of when I'd get down to my last few pieces while playing checkers as a kid. I would move them up and then move them back. I knew that there was a chance I would lose if I kept moving forward, so I would play it safe over and over and over again. Guess what? That didn't get me anywhere in the game and it doesn't get us anywhere in life. Having an obedient heart means trusting God enough to say YES. Even when you don't see all of the parts or understand the why behind what He has asked you to do. It's not easy, but I want to share some moments where God has shown me the fruit from being obedient even when I didn't understand.

Having an obedient heart means trusting God enough to say YES.

1. IT'S HARD TO OBEY WHEN GOD ASKS ME TO DO SOMETHING WEIRD

I can't tell you how many times God has given me a weird assignment. At first, I usually shake my head and laugh because none of it makes any sense to me. After that, I try to ignore it because nothing in me wants to do something that is going to make me look weird or make someone else feel weird. However, I have learned that when God says do something He will usually not let up until I do it. A few years ago, I was in my car driving kids during a very heated moment. I was personally carrying a lot mentally, and one of the kids I was driving was suffering from extreme anxiety. Sometimes, I find myself in spiritual places where the burden is so heavy I don't know what to do. I felt so heavy that day as I was praying in my head over and over while going down the highway. I knew I was fighting against the Enemy through prayer, but I wasn't prepared for what God would ask me to do next. I know you're probably going to think I am crazy, but there was no doubt in my mind that I heard God on that highway. He told me to pull the car over into a parking lot and walk around the car seven times while praying for the Enemy to flee. What in the world?

I knew I was going to look like I was crazy, not to mention what I would tell the kids that were in my car that day. I could have navigated that a little easier if it had just been my kids, but that wasn't the case. I had about four minutes to decide if I was going to be obedient or not. Thankfully, I said yes. I am not sure if I was more scared about what people were going to think or having to explain my behavior to the kids' parents. Either way, I was coming unglued inside. With each lap, I prayed and felt more peace. I am not going to lie and say I walked proudly around that car. There were a few laps where I was in a lunge position hoping that the kids would think I was checking my tires or something more normal. I was tempted to stop after five laps, but I knew in my heart that God had said seven. So, seven it was. I did my laps, got back in the car, and kept driving. To this day, I am not even sure if the kids were paying attention or if they were just too scared to ask, but the whole situation was never discussed.

God directs us with a purpose.

It wasn't until later when God showed me the why behind this act of obedience. He used Joshua and the story of Jericho to teach me that He cares about the details when He asks us to do something. God had instructed Joshua to have his people march around the walls of Jericho seven times on the seventh day. I fully believe that if they had stopped at five they would not have seen God move in the way that He did. Many times, our fears or lack of confidence cause us to stop short when we are walking out of obedience. I can think of many times where I have gotten going and the level of discomfort caused me to pull back and not follow through. We have to trust that if God gives us details then we need to do as He says. If God says to give $100, then giving $99 is disobedience. God directs us with a purpose. No matter how weird it seems or feels, we need to walk out the steps in the way He instructed us to. I have seen that the more weird it feels, the more God shows up in the process! So just remember, it's okay to do weird things when your obedience is on the line!

2. BEING OBEDIENT WHEN I CAN'T SEE THE WHOLE PICTURE OR UNDERSTAND THE WHY IS VERY DIFFICULT FOR ME.

My mind can't help but go back to the old Garth Brooks song, "Unanswered Prayers." It is so true when it says, "Some of God's greatest gifts are unanswered prayers." I can remember being a high school girl, and even a college girl, and begging for God to help "that one boy" like me or think I was pretty. I thought I knew what I needed or how it would make me feel to be liked by certain people, but I had no idea what I needed. I was clueless and was praying for things that I thought would make me feel complete. I praise God for so many unanswered prayers. I can only imagine where I would be if He had answered some of those.

Sometimes, I still feel like the same young girl running around trying to get all the pieces of my life to fit in the way that I see it best. I fully understand the unknown factors of life, but I still fight the urge to tell God how I think things should go. Learning to trust God when He only gives you part of the puzzle is kind of like walking into a blind date. You may know one or two things about the person, but the unknown can drive us crazy. I have to tell myself over and over that God sees the whole puzzle and can see how this one tiny piece of obedience is going to fit so perfectly. We can either trust or not trust, but I have seen so much spiritual maturity when I say yes blindfolded. It's okay to pray, "God, I have no idea why you are asking me to do this and I am scared to death, but I blindly say yes to you." Trusting with that mindset will grow you in a way you can't even imagine, but it takes setting aside all of our fleshly tendencies in order to do it. Your obedience could be something as simple as deleting an app off of your phone or something big like moving away to make a kingdom impact. Regardless of the step, I can assure you that it is an important step in your faith. You will be shocked once you do see the whole picture and all the beauty that came from that first blindfolded step.

3. IT'S IMPORTANT TO BE OBEDIENT, EVEN WHEN I DON'T WANT TO!

Let's be honest, we are selfish people who like things our way in the comfort of our homes. Choosing to be uncomfortable is just not something that we do often, but I recently heard a quote that has really shifted the way I think. It said, "We need to get comfortable with being uncomfortable." Many of my yeses to obedience were uncomfortable, but some of those moments were extremely pivotal points in my journey. There is something powerful about choosing to abandon our flesh and what feels good in the moment. It's easy to stay where you're at, which is why so many find themselves stuck in their comfortable place. It's funny because many are not happy with where they are at, whether it be their health, their marriage, or their job, but most people are not willing to do what they need to do to change it. Our unhealthy ways can feel comfortable, so we stay in the cycle because we know what to expect.

There is something powerful about choosing to abandon our flesh and what feels good in the moment.

The one thing that stretches me and really pushes me to grow is when I choose to say yes to something that I don't want to do. For years, I told God I would never write a book because the last thing I wanted to do was humble myself to the vulnerable place it would take for me to put things on paper. I didn't want everyone knowing my business. Just recently, He burdened my heart to delete Instagram until this book was complete. I fought that for almost six weeks because I didn't want to miss out on updates or what was going on in other people's lives. I pushed and pushed because I just didn't want to do it. Over the years, He has asked me to move in areas where I was a hard no and has shown me that my hard no always came down to a heart issue inside of me. I remember saying, "I will never homeschool my kids," and here I am in the midst of a school where my kids are home half of the week. Brandon and I both agree that it was the best move we could have ever made for our family, yet there I was telling God I wouldn't even consider it. Man, I would have missed out! We tell God we will say yes to most things, but then we make sure He knows where we don't want to budge. Let me give you a little secret. The hardest no's usually come from areas we need to be pushed and stretched in, so be careful of those hard no's! Before you know it, you'll be writing a book or doing exactly the thing that was on the top of your hard no list.

Once you realize that this life is not about you or what you want, the more you will live with the eyes of Jesus.

The stronger we grow in our faith, the more we will be faced with choosing our faith over our flesh. I have found that having both is not an option. The Bible is clear in Galatians 5:16 when it says we must walk in the Spirit so that we don't give in to the desires of our flesh. Once you realize that this life is not about you or what you want, the more you will live with the eyes of Jesus. You will start to see the things that Jesus sees, and your heart will break for the things that break His heart. The only way to become more like Him is to be obedient in the moments when your flesh is screaming not to! Dying to our flesh will change us and grow our confidence in the right things that will make a kingdom impact.

I am still learning how to live with a more obedient heart. I want to be less like the girl that does everything Google says and more like the girl who says yes to God without hesitation. How do we get there? Just like everything else: baby steps.

PROCESS AND REFLECT:

- Is it tough for you to be obedient when God asks you to do something?
- If you said yes, write down the reasons it is hard for you. (Are you unsure if it's God? Are you worried about what someone might think? Fear?)

17

chapter seventeen: the ugly sister

"Let the words of my mouth and the meditations of my heart be pleasing to you, O Lord."

PSALM 19:14

Does anyone remember the old song, “O Be Careful, Little Eyes?” I remember my mom and my Mimi singing that song to me over and over when I was little. I vividly remember hearing the words of the song play in my mind when I was older trying to debate a movie or decide whether or not I wanted to go to the haunted house with the other kids. When my mom would sing the song, she would tell me that once I see something, I can’t unsee it; once I hear something, I can’t unhear it; and once I say something, I can’t unsay it. The older I got, the more I saw this play out in my own life, which is why I believed every word she taught me. It only takes one scary movie to keep you up with nightmares, and none of us forget when someone we love lashes out at us using hurtful words. There were many times growing up that I wished that I had a big eraser to undo some of the things I saw, heard, and said. Unfortunately, there was no fix in many of those situations. Those situations usually turned into life lessons or long-term hurts that built up inside of me.

Not only is it sad and sinful, but there is so much power in our words to either make or break a person.

We have all heard bible verses about our words and how they can make or break a situation, yet there are so many times we let them fly out of our mouths as if we have never been taught what’s right. As I go throughout my week, I am shocked at the way I hear kids speak to their parents while I am standing right there or how adults speak to one another on a Facebook page. Every single one of us knows what it feels like to be made fun of or put down, so why do we allow our own mouths to be the source of pain for another person? Not only is it sad and sinful, but there is so much power in our words to either make or break a person.

When I was younger, I never really felt good at anything. Sure, I made good grades and I was a good kid, but I never felt like I stood out like other kids did. I struggled with my weight, I was usually picked last for the Red Rover game in PE, and I was insecure with the way I looked. My sister has always been my very best friend, and she still is, but growing up alongside her wasn't always easy because she was so good at everything. She was thin, an athlete, and a cheerleader. I guess you could say I always felt inferior to her, but I was always able to separate those feelings and still have a very healthy relationship with her. Looking back, I know that was God's protection over us because that could have easily caused division. Instead, our hearts have always been bonded. I know my mom played a big role as well by always making sure we felt seen and beautiful. My mom never allowed ugly words like stupid, shut-up, or name calling to be said in our home, so we rarely heard hurtful words. The only hurtful words in my mind were my own thoughts if that makes sense.

I guess you could say I grew out of the comparison mindset as I pursued my own health. Before I knew it, it was no longer a thing I struggled with. It wasn't until I was about 38 years old when I finally had a label for the mindset I had growing up. I was standing in my kitchen talking to a lady that had known me my entire life. In a casual conversation, she said, "I was talking to someone the other day about you and we were saying how you were the ugly sister when you and Audra were kids." Talk about a punch in the gut. All these years later, after I had done the hard work to find my own identity and get to a healthy mindset, it still hurt. Half of me wanted to cry and the other half of me wanted to punch her in the face. I mean, who says something like that?

I had struggled my whole childhood to fight those thoughts, but I had never used those two words to describe what I was feeling. That day, not only did she reopen a wound that I thought had healed, but she gave me a new label that the Enemy would now have for ammunition to use against me. The ugly sister. It felt so harsh, so permanent. Ironically, I was leading a boot camp retreat with my sister that evening, and I was able to tell her what happened so that she could help me fight against those words. I love that God orchestrated that timing for us. Audra is my spiritual prayer partner. She's the one I run to in moments when I need help fighting through prayer and intercession. I knew that none of this was about Audra and all of it was an arrow the Enemy had thrown my way to get me off track. If you are anything like me, words matter so much. Words of affirmation is my top love language, which can be a blessing and a curse. When that lady told me I was the ugly sister, I learned that I wasn't going to make it if I allowed other people's humanness to define me. I had to decide what words I was going to listen to and choose to forget the rest.

I can't make someone else be kind or hold their tongue in a disagreement, but I can hold my tongue when everything inside of me is raging.

It was important for me to start with this story because I want you to see that all of us carry around a bag of words that have been said to us along the way. We wrestle with them, we believe them, we pray against them, and then we believe them again. It's a cycle that is hard to escape, especially if the words keep coming our way. I have learned two things when it comes to words. I am the only one that can control what I do with the words spoken to me and I am the only one who can control the words that come out of my mouth. I can't make someone else be kind or hold their tongue in a disagreement, but I can hold my tongue when everything inside of me is raging. Let me fill you in on a little secret. The Holy Spirit is the only one who has ever provided me the self-control to hold my tongue. When I fail with my words, it is because I have failed to ask the Holy Spirit for help. I think we can all agree that self-control over the mouth is a battle we face daily, no matter how old we are. In James, it says, "Yet if we are able to bridle the words we say, we are powerful enough to control ourselves in every way, and that means our character is mature and fully developed." God knew our tongues would be difficult to manage, but He is telling us that if we can discipline our tongue then we are capable of self-discipline in every other area of our lives. This is huge!

We have six people who live in this house and our words have always been a priority when it comes to the way we parent. Maybe it's because of my baggage with being hurt by others' words, who knows, but Brandon and I care very much about how our family speaks to one another. You want to see me flip out and lose my mind? Show up on a day when one of the kids has used their mouth to hurt someone else in the house. I am extremely calm and patient until I hear ugly words. That's when Mama goes crazy! It hurts my heart so much and the kids see the way it affects me. I want to share two things that I share with my kids often so that they don't make the same mistakes as I did. My desire is for them to be wiser and kinder than me, and the best way to achieve that goal is for them to learn from all the times I dropped the ball.

1. SOMETIMES IT'S BETTER TO JUST KEEP YOUR MOUTH SHUT.

The Bible is full of so much wisdom. One of the best chunks of wisdom is found in James when it tells us to be slow to speak. If I could choose one key verse to follow it would be James 1:19: "Be quick to listen, slow to speak, and slow to anger." The times I have chosen to live out this verse are no doubt some of the most peaceful times in my life. On the flip side, I have been full of regret when I have spoken too quickly without thinking. No doubt about it. If you're a teenager reading this, it's okay to hear your parents out and just be quiet in your response. If you're a married person, it's actually very helpful in a situation to really listen while your spouse is talking instead of planning your comeback in your head.

We don't lose anything by being patient in our reactions or responses, but we always risk relational damage when we don't think before speaking. It's the simplest nugget of wisdom that people fail to take advantage of. We wonder why relationships are tense and marriages are failing. It's because we think that what we have to say is more important than the person standing in front of us. That is not ever the case. If we don't protect our people with our words, then one day we'll look back and we may not have those people. We have to understand that if we don't choose self-control with our words then we can't blame anyone but ourselves if they walk away.

We don't lose anything by being patient in our reactions or responses, but we always risk relational damage when we don't think before speaking.

I have always been very quick to speak or react, but I have intentionally made an effort to be better in this area over the last few years. I have realized that not only does it keep me from hurting someone else with my words, but it saves me so much emotional energy because I am not igniting a fire with my words. Instead, I am diffusing it. I tell my kids to count to 10 (or more) in their heads before responding in a heated conversation. I remind them it's okay to take a time out and give themselves a few minutes to regroup. Choose to pause so that your brain can catch up and you can avoid adding negative fuel to the relational fire. This takes maturity, this takes practice, and this will most definitely take the Holy Spirit working in and through you!

2. DON'T SAY OR TEXT ANYTHING YOU DON'T WANT THE WHOLE WORLD TO HEAR OR READ

This was a hard lesson for me that was awkward, embarrassing, and nerve-wracking all at the same time. It was a special moment at the age of 43. I know, I know, that wasn't too long ago. It was a Saturday morning and I felt like I had already been put through the ringer. On this rough morning, I found myself in the parking lot of a donut store. I love glazed donuts but sugar is my biggest enemy when it comes to battling RA. I know that if I choose to eat sugar then I will almost always suffer, so it's always a conscious decision when I eat a donut. That morning I was already in pain, so after about five minutes of staring at the entrance to the donut shop I drove away. I felt so powerful in that moment because I just said NO to my biggest temptation. I thought it would be funny to send my friend, Casey, a text about my morning.

The text said, "I am losing it over here. I either need a donut, a margarita, or some good sex! Maybe all three!" Yes ma'am, I did. I wasn't ready for what unfolded next. As soon as I hit send, something in me just didn't feel right. I immediately picked up the phone to call and warn her that it was a more private text. Unfortunately, I was too late. Casey informed me that as soon as she got my text, she clicked on it to tell her car to read it over the speaker. Yes, friends, her car read it over the speaker with her child in the car. I told you it was a special moment for me, ugh! All I remember is saying I was sorry over and over while I was literally dying inside. There is a meme that says "Put me on speaker at your own risk!" This was definitely written for me!

For years, I had told my kids to never text something that you don't want other parents, your pastor, or your grandmother reading. Here I was breaking my own rule! Trust me, I felt every bit of that poor decision. Of course, Casey handled it so gracefully, but it definitely made an impact on me. In this day and age, it is way too easy to screenshot, to let others secretly listen in on a call, or to accidentally text something private to the wrong person or group. Don't risk it! I feel like this is one of those rules that you only break once and you learn fast! Practice self-control in the moments you just want to vent about someone else and ask yourself how it's going to feel if the wrong person were to read it. More times than not, I can assure you that you will choose to not send the text. You can't take it back after it's read and the consequences of it all will make you feel yucky inside. Going back to my little childhood song, here is a new line for all of us living life in 2024: "O be careful little fingers what you text!"

PROCESS AND REFLECT:

- On a scale from 1-10, 10 being a good job, how well do you control the words that come out of your mouth?
- Who in your life do you feel suffers the most when you fail to control your tongue? Be specific. It could be one person or several people.

18

chapter eighteen: hurdles

"Therefore, since we are surrounded by such a great cloud of witnesses, let us throw off everything that hinders and the sin that so easily entangles. And let us run with perseverance the race marked out for us, fixing our eyes on Jesus, the perfecter of our faith."

HEBREWS 12:1-2

You know how I told you that I was never really good at anything athletic growing up? Well, that was true, but for some reason I decided to be on the track team my junior year of high school. I am certain that there wasn't a tryout or else I wouldn't have made the team. Maybe they needed more runners that year, who knows. Either way, I signed up. I loved all the team aspects of wearing the team uniform and the sweats that went over it. I think it made me feel like I was someone important. There's something about being part of a group that we can all relate to. Maybe it was the feeling of being included or known, but let me just tell you that I absolutely loved being a part of the team. I knew I was probably the slowest one out there, but I didn't care because I was showing up and doing something I enjoyed.

The day came for my first track meet. I had chosen to run hurdles. For the life of me, I can't figure out who thought that would be a good idea, but that was the situation I found myself in. I remember being so excited. Even sitting here right now, I can remember how I felt right before the race. I was ready to try my very best, but I had zero experience with any of it. Having to put my feet in the blocks at the starting line threw me off, but I managed to get myself situated. I remember the coach telling us one thing that I will never forget. He said, "Run your race, look straight ahead, and don't look at the other runners."

You would think I would have been able to follow simple directions, seeing as how I was such a rule follower at that age, but I completely blew it when the race started. I had made it through about half of the hurdles when I decided to look beside me to see how close the other runner was. I knew I wasn't in last at that point and couldn't fight the urge to see how close she was to catching me. Not but one second later, my back foot hit the hurdle, I flew headfirst towards the track, and my track season was over before it even started. I was hurt, I was bleeding a lot, and I was humiliated. Here's the thing, it takes a lot to put yourself out there when you're not good at something. It's even harder to get back up and try again when you literally fall on your face. As a 16-year-old girl who was already battling deep insecurity, I didn't have it in me to try again. I never went back and I quit the team.

It sounds like a crappy story—trust me, it was—but I learned so much through that experience. I didn't fully process all of it at the time, but over the years God has allowed this moment in my life to resurface to teach me lessons along the way. Here are three lessons I learned that I hope will encourage you to run your "race" well.

1. WE CAN'T MOVE FORWARD IF WE ARE LOOKING BEHIND US

It doesn't matter what it is, taking the time to turn around will cause you to lose your focus. The minute we take our eyes off of where they need to be, we open the door for the Enemy to creep in and start having his way in our minds. For me, the physical hurdle was an obvious one. I think we can all see why I fell down. Other life hurdles I have faced have often been camouflaged, which caused me to stumble or even fall. Proverbs 4:25-27 specifically tells us to fix our gaze and to not look to the right or to the left. The Lord knows our natural tendencies and the consequences of them.

The minute we take our eyes off of where they need to be, we open the door for the Enemy to creep in and start having his way in our minds.

If you keep turning to look at your past, then I can promise you that it won't end up well for you. Yes, learn from your mistakes, but your mistakes do not define you! Every single time you look back, you're adding another hurdle in your path that will continue to cause you to stumble. Over time, the hurdles build up and you will have created an even more difficult road to overcome. The memories of our past are hard enough, but looking back adds shame, guilt, insecurities, and fear to our minds. If you have asked for forgiveness and made it right, then fix your eyes on Jesus and let yourself have another chance at living. Living in the past is not the way God desires us to live.

2. COMPARING YOUR RACE TO SOMEONE ELSE'S ISN'T FAIR TO YOU OR TO THEM

There came a point in my life where this finally clicked in my mind and I was able to see other women the way God sees them. We live in a world right now where everything is put out there and it can feel impossible not to compare. I get it, it's hard! However, it's also hard when you're living with a brain that looks at everyone else to define your own worth. I read something that has really helped me in this area of comparison and with having a judgemental heart: "Comparing yourself to others will either make you feel better about yourself or worse about yourself, neither honor God." This statement hit me hard because I want to honor God. Comparing ourselves to others is a huge struggle within all of us as women. Maybe you're not the jealous type and you don't struggle with comparison, but feeling better than someone else is also a heart issue that needs to be addressed.

Each of our races are filled with hurdles, some that are seen by the world and some that we choose to keep private. It's unfair to compare yourself to someone else because your hurdles may not be the same and your experiences have you in different places. It's like a 40-year-old trying to compare her skin to a 20-year-old. That's never going to be fair because 20 years of life ages a person. Whether it's something physical, your marriage, or your sin struggles, the roads we have walked are different. It's not fair to put yourself up against someone else. It's certainly not fair to them because we usually show jealous or yucky feelings to the other person when we compare. Trust me, it's always a losing situation, so work hard to be the best version of yourself regardless of who is around you.

3. GETTING OUT OF YOUR LANE LEADS TO CONFLICT

My eldest daughter, Brylee, is learning to drive right now. Yesterday, we were driving down a semi-busy street near our house and she kept crossing over the lane. She wasn't in the other lane, but the edge of the car was. I immediately yelled, "Woah, you have to stay in your lane!" Here's the thing, those lanes are there for a reason. Their sole purpose is to keep a wreck from happening and provide boundaries for everyone on the road. For Brylee, getting out of her lane could lead to a mild side swipe or it could lead to a full-on dangerous collision. Life works in the same way. There are times when I have gotten out of my lane, but the resulting conflict was mild and an apology was sufficient in order to move forward. However, there have been other times when getting out of my lane ended up being a domino effect that hurt many people.

Staying in my lane applies to marriage as well. It took Brandon and I about 15 years of marriage before we both embraced this idea, "Just worry about yourself!" We learned that if we both worry about ourselves and strive to be our personal best then we are better together. We wasted too many years looking at each other instead of looking in the mirror. It seems like the blame game is the natural response for most humans. We become so quick to point fingers and point out how someone could do things better. What if we asked ourselves how we could be better? I think we would all be pleasantly surprised at the outcome when we work on the things in our own lane.

4. WHEN SOMEONE WITH EXPERIENCE GIVES YOU WISE ADVICE, YOU SHOULD LISTEN

When I think about my fall on the track that day, I can't help but wonder how things would have played out had I listened to the coach. I think about how cool it would have been for me to find a team and a sport that I could have stayed a part of. Maybe I would have stayed active and not put on 50 pounds during college. I wonder how not listening to someone that knew better could have saved me the embarrassment I felt that day.

There is always someone that knows more than us and who has walked many of the hard roads that we will face in our lives. Maybe we have authority issues or maybe we are stubborn, but I sure wish I would have listened to a few key people that God undoubtedly put in my life for a reason. The whole track deal was minor compared to real life trials that we walk through on a daily basis. I have learned to listen when someone gives me wisdom. I wish I could say that it didn't take failure and hitting rock bottom for me to learn to listen, but I am thankful I listen now. I promise you one thing, listening to others who are seeking Jesus and have walked the road you're walking will keep you from so much pain.

No one has the ability to understand the layers of pain from sexual sin until you choose it and walk that road for yourself.

I think about the high school and college girls reading this. I am sure that you have been told that sex before marriage will have pain and consequences. I realize that it is hard to listen to that advice when you feel like you are in love or you're missing out on what everyone else is doing. I get it. When I was your age, I was that same girl battling the same thing in my mind. It's unfortunate that all it takes is one mess up for you to see the truth and wish you had listened to everyone who told you that sex is worth waiting for. Sex is one of those areas where God is so crystal clear because the repercussions from sexual sin cut deep. Whether you're a teen girl deciding that you want to have sex before marriage or a married woman debating going outside of your marriage, I urge you to listen to the wisdom you have been told regarding this issue. Sexual sin not only hurts our hearts deeply, but it wounds the hearts of those around us. No one has the ability to understand the layers of pain from sexual sin until you choose it and walk that road for yourself. I believe this is why so many try to warn against sexual sin because they don't want anyone else to hurt in the ways that they did. I have never met a teenage girl or woman that hasn't regretted the sexual sin she found herself in. When it comes to this, you either trust the wisdom or you learn the hard way. You're the only one who can decide which way you are going to choose.

I will leave you with this thought: All of the hurdles we face are simply distractions the Enemy throws at us in an attempt to take our eyes off the Lord.

I will leave you with this thought: All of the hurdles we face are simply distractions the Enemy throws at us in an attempt to take our eyes off the Lord. He knows if he can get us to compare ourselves or look back at our past then he will ultimately have us living for the wrong audience. I tell myself all the time "Don't let the Enemy win here" and it's a great thing to remind yourself every single time you start to look anywhere but up!

PROCESS AND REFLECT:

- What are the hurdles you face in your daily life? (these could be physical hurdles, emotional hurdles, mental hurdles, spiritual hurdles, etc)
- What things from the past cause you to stumble or slow down as you are trying to move forward?

19

chapter nineteen: indomitable spirit

"Do not grow weary in doing good, for in due time we will reap a harvest if we don't give up."

GALATIANS 6:9

Brandon and I were married five years before we attempted to think about having children. The two of us fully agreed that we had a lot of learning to do before trying to learn how to be parents. During those last few years when it was just the two of us, we lived near Oklahoma City. Brandon spent three years serving as a dentist in the Air Force while I spent my days teaching 7th grade science. I guess you could say we were learning to be adults, but I was so far from understanding who I was as a woman, much less a wife. It's funny because looking back now I realize how far I needed to come, but I had no idea at the time.

During those difficult years, I signed up to try out a cardio kickboxing class at the karate studio near my house. I honestly think I was just looking for something to do at night to keep busy, plus the workout part of it was appealing. Each week, I would show up to take the class and I really loved the design of the program. When my fitness class would end, the karate class would begin. I loved seeing all the students, young and old, come in with their different colored belts around their waist. Over time, I became very interested in the whole idea of karate. Before I knew it, I was a 27-year-old walking in with a white belt tied around my waist. The whole thing was very unusual because I had never even entertained the idea of taking karate, but there was something about walking into the class that felt right.

Slowly but surely, I was able to change my belt color after passing each test. Next thing I knew, I was one step away from my black belt. It was weird because when you're standing there with a white belt on it almost seems like an impossible dream to get to black. However, once you start taking steps, you realize that maybe you really can make it a reality. About a year into the program, I decided that I didn't want to have children until I accomplished my goal of becoming a black belt. From that moment on, I lived and breathed karate. I would work as a teacher all day and spend my nights training for as long as I could in order to reach my goal.

I can still remember standing in that gym, the day of my big black belt test, shaking from head to toe. I knew I had a long day ahead of me if I wanted to go home with a black belt around my waist. To give you an idea, a black belt test has many different rounds and takes nearly all day to finish. Unsurprisingly, I did very well with my forms and kicks tests. I had practiced those elements for countless hours, so I felt confident during that part of the test.

The real fear hit right before I started my sparring rounds. I knew I had to fight 14 rounds, with the last two being against senior black belts. You have to remember, I had been testing all day and was very exhausted, while these fighters came in fresh each round. It wasn't a fair fight, but that was how it was designed to be. In sparring, the rounds are two minutes each and you're allowed to hit the other one anywhere you want. By the time I got to round 10, I was done. The hits were constant all over my body. I had been punched in the head, face, ribs, and shins. I honestly didn't have much left by that point and knew that the senior black belts would be coming in to attack hard! As I was fighting the fearful tears, not to mention pure exhaustion, one of the other black belts pulled me aside and said a few words my spirit needed to hear in order to keep going.

He said, "You have already proven yourself all day long. At this point, your goal is not to win the match. No one is expecting that. In these last few rounds, they are testing your heart. They want to know if you have what it takes to keep fighting when you have nothing left. They want to know if you are going to quit and walk away or if your heart will push through." I knew right then that I would be okay because I knew my heart would never give up. I told myself at that moment that I wasn't going to quit, no matter how much it hurt, even if that meant they would have to carry me out when it was over. I had been in a place of experiencing extreme pain before when I ran that half marathon with a bleeding ulcer, remember? I knew I could do it because I had done it before. It's funny how God allowed me to walk through two very physical moments where my body was broken down so much to prepare me for the emotional battles that would later come my way. The truth is, I would always choose the physical pain over the emotional pain, but what God showed me was that my spirit would be the key force that would drive me to the finish line in all the difficult situations life would throw my way.

Sure enough, I went straight from the black belt test to the hospital because I was so beat up and dehydrated, but you better believe I had that black belt tied around my waist when the test was over. I knew it was too much for my sweet mom to watch that day, but she was right beside me at the hospital. She understood my heart in needing to do whatever it took to finish. I have always been aware that I would never be the best at anything and that was okay because there would never be a person who could compete with my indomitable spirit.

My spirit and my heart belonged to me. They define an indomitable spirit as a spirit that cannot be beaten or defeated. During that black belt test, I was the only one who could decide what kind of spirit I was going to have. I chose perseverance in the face of fear. God used that test to prove to me that I could push through any pain or any circumstances if I didn't lose my spirit. From that moment on, I held onto that indomitable spirit and it has been the driving force over the last 20 years as I have fought depression, pain, marriage battles, a physical diagnosis, and everything in between.

When Jesus has the wheel and I have a willing spirit, I have seen the Holy Spirit take over in beautiful ways.

I am living proof that a person can fight any battle if the power of Jesus is driving the car! I am sure we have all sung "Jesus Take the Wheel" over the years, but think about what those words truly mean. When Jesus has the wheel and we release our controlling hands off of the situation, then and only then can we trust that we will be okay. When Jesus has the wheel and

I have a willing spirit, I have seen the Holy Spirit take over in beautiful ways. Most of us have the equation wrong and cling to the wheel. I sure did for many years, but when you get right, and let go of the wheel, you will experience a peace that passes all understanding. I wanted to leave you with a few final thoughts.

1. MANY THINGS WILL FIGHT YOU IN AN EFFORT TO STEAL YOUR SPIRIT

You have an Enemy that loves to steal anything good inside of you. He wants your peace, he wants your friendships, he wants your identity, and he wants your eternity. Matter of fact, theft and destruction is his sole purpose. Choosing Jesus won't keep the Enemy from trying to work or pursue your heart, but the Holy Spirit is the weapon that can be used in this fight for your spirit. Time and time again, I can assure you that the Enemy thought he had me, but where there is a will, with the Holy Spirit, there's a way. The Enemy can't steal your spirit unless you let him. Even when I think of the darkest times in my life when my spirit was running on 1%, I could always see a tiny ray of light and knew I had to keep going and seek the help of the Holy Spirit. You get to decide where you stand with Jesus and the authority you have over the Enemy. As for me, I now stand in victory with the Holy Spirit.

2. OUR SPIRIT WILL NOT ONLY BE THE DRIVING FORCE TO HELP PUSH US THROUGH, BUT OUR SPIRIT WILL OFTENTIMES INTERRUPT CRUCIAL MOMENTS WHEN WE NEED A WAY OUT

The convictions I have held throughout my life have definitely been tested over the last 43 years. No matter how hard I tried to do the right thing, I can remember all of the times I found myself in compromising situations. It's like I knew in my heart I needed a way out, but

I needed help knowing how to get out. When I was a senior in high school, there was a night where I can clearly remember my spirit interrupting my efforts as I made some really poor decisions.

Up until that point, I had stayed on the path that I planned. I had never been drunk, I had never lied to my parents, I had committed to waiting until marriage to have sex, and I had very clear boundaries that had kept me on the path. In August of my senior year, my friend Brittany and I came up with this plan to have a sleepover with our boyfriends while her parents were out of town. Neither of us had any intention of crossing any big lines. We just wanted a little freedom. Somehow, we managed to get all four of us to her house without it being on our parents' radar. It started off fun with swimming and hanging out, but sometime around midnight, something didn't feel right in my spirit. I wasn't technically doing anything wrong (besides not telling my parents the truth), but the conviction in my spirit was screaming inside of me to the point where I was physically sick. I had put myself in a compromising situation where the boundaries were not clear and had opened the door to the Enemy. I needed a way out and I knew it deep in my soul.

Not more than a few hours later, news broke on the TV that Princess Diana had been involved in a terrible car accident that she did not survive. You can imagine as all four of us laid on pallets on the living room floor with our eyes glued to the TV. We didn't have phones or social media back then, so we had to wait patiently as the details surfaced. I will never forget when they announced that "due to extremely high speeds, Princess Diana did not survive the crash." The distraction of the tragedy not only gave me a way out from falling into sin, but God opened my eyes to the consequences of putting yourself in a situation with unclear boundaries. Had her car not been going way above the speed limit, she may have survived. As a 17-year-old girl who was trying to stand strong in my convictions, this night made an impact on me for

The day you
decide to get
up and fight is
the day you will
overcome the
mountains in
your life.

a long time. Teens and women, you won't slip into sin if you don't put yourself in situations that could lead you to a vulnerable place. Yes, my spirit interrupted my evening and got my attention that night, but I shouldn't have even been there to begin with. So many times we make our lives and decisions so much harder because we put ourselves in places we were never meant to be in.

3. YOUR SPIRIT IS YOURS AND IT'S ON YOU TO STAY TRUE TO IT

We live in a world where we don't want to do the hard work, we want someone else to fix it, and we want the easy way out. When it comes to deciding whether you are going to fight for your marriage, friendships, children, or health, you have to be the one to do the work. When I would help women on their weight loss journey, I would always say, "I can't get up and do the workout for you and I can't take the cookie out of your mouth. I can motivate and guide you, but self-discipline is on you!" The day you decide to get up and fight is the day you will overcome the mountains in your life. It is going to be hard and uncomfortable at first, but it's impossible to get to the other side without getting uncomfortable.

Discomfort and work is part of the process. If achieving the goal of a black belt was easy and comfortable, then I would have missed out on all of the many lessons and growth through the process. I not only grew physically, but I took massive steps in overcoming an insecurity I had lived with my whole life. When we walk through the process of being uncomfortable, we appreciate being on the other side even more. However, step one is taking responsibility and accepting the fact that you have to be the one to do the work. Until you have fought a hard fight with an indomitable spirit, you are missing out on one of the greatest gifts known as restoration. When God restores, it's a beautiful thing that changes everyone in the process.

I will leave you with the words that were said to me in that final round of my sparring.

These words fit well with any battle! "You have already proven yourself all day long. At this point, your goal is not to win the match. No one is expecting that. In these last few rounds, they are testing your heart. They want to know if you have what it takes to keep fighting when you have nothing left. They want to know if you are going to quit and walk away or if your heart will push through."

PROCESS AND REFLECT:

- Think about the condition of your spirit. Is your heart beating strong for the Lord and is your spirit aligned with His desires? Are you struggling because you haven't been fueling your spiritual tank well?

20

chapter twenty: be the bridge

"If any of you lack wisdom, you should ask God, who gives generously to all without finding fault, and it will be given to you."

JAMES 1:5

I have never been a daredevil in any way. I have a healthy amount of fear, sometimes too much fear, so taking dangerous risks for fun was never my thing…except this one time. I can probably count on one hand, maybe two, all of the very dumb things I have done in my life. The one I am about to share with you is near the top of the list, no doubt. To this day, I wonder how I lived through it. I grew up in Grand Prairie, Texas, near a lake called Joe Pool Lake. If you are reading this and you are from the area, there is a possibility you may have made this risky decision just like I did. If you have read all the chapters so far and not skipped any, you have probably gathered that my youth group friends and I weren't very experienced with all the crazy things. I chalk this poor decision up to boredom or maybe an attempt to do something "bad" without being bad. Who knows, but for whatever reason, a few of us headed out to Joe Pool Lake one night to be risk-takers. If you are reading this Mom and Dad, I am so sorry for being so stupid. Trust me, I have thanked God over and over for not letting me die because of my stupidity.

We had heard that some kids from our school had gone bridge jumping out at Joe Pool Lake after dark. When I heard about it, it sounded like a fun thing to do that might give us a little bit of a rush. It took us about 20 minutes to walk out to the spot where kids would jump. I thought I was going to puke when we got there. We were well aware we would be in trouble by the cops if we got caught, so we had to wait until it was very late before we went out by the water. We had to jump from the actual road. There wasn't a ledge off the side like I had imagined in my head. It was pitch black and cars were flying down the road as we made our way to the top jumping area of the bridge. I swear it felt like one of those crime shows where someone is trying to run from the cops and they are staring over a dark bridge that only leads to water. The bridge was about 40 feet high and I can still remember what it felt like looking down to the water. I am not sure what was worse, the unknown of what it would feel like to hit the water or the unknown of what was in the water below.

Brandon and I were good friends at the time, so he was there too. He jumped before me though, whereas I stood there shaking like a leaf for what seemed like forever. Then, I finally jumped. I would say it was about 11:00 PM the first time I ever jumped. I screamed the entire way down. It felt like I was never going to hit the water. The worst part was submerging so deep and trying to get up to the surface. It was the scariest thing I had ever done. I am not going to lie, the rush of the whole experience was amazing, but every time I think back to the night I shake my head at my stupidity. If any of my four children ever decide to jump off that bridge, I feel like I would literally lose my mind! I currently only live about 15 minutes from that bridge and probably drive over it at least once a month. Every single time I pass that spot, I hold my breath because all the fear of the night rushes back over me. It was definitely an unforgettable experience.

Some bridges will bring life and fruit, while other bridges will bring pain and suffering.

The more I write in this book, the more I feel like Abraham, and all of his tests and failures in his life. So, what did He teach me from bridge jumping? He taught me not to be an idiot! Just kidding, it's deeper than that. The longer I live, the more I have felt God ask me to be obedient to jump off some life bridges that were scary. Any time we are facing the unknown and God says move, it's a scary thing on so many levels. As we go throughout our lives, we will be faced with bridges we should freely jump off of and bridges we should run from. No matter the bridge in front of us, we should always think before we jump because every jump will be followed with something. Some bridges will bring life and fruit, while other bridges will bring pain and suffering. I got lucky when I jumped off of a bridge that night, it could have ended in so much suffering. Unfortunately, I have also jumped off bridges that have led me to hit rock bottom in the worst ways. Once you jump, the decision is made.

You may be reading this while you are feeling the pain of your yes to jump; I am so very sorry because I know exactly how you feel. Or maybe you're staring over the edge, knowing you are one step away from taking the leap, debating whether you want to jump into sin. I want you to know that making the decision to jump shouldn't be one you take lightly. It could be something that feels small, like gossiping in a friend group or being tempted to click on that website you know isn't good for you. It could also be sex before marriage or sex outside of your marriage. These types of jumps are typically like quicksand and we lose control before we know it. Maybe for you, it is a technology jump or a pornography jump. Remember what we said about our eyes? Once we "go there" and see things we are not meant to see, it's almost like a videotape that will play in our mind and we will struggle relentlessly to make it stop.

Once we "go there" and see things we are not meant to see, it's almost like a videotape that will play in our mind and we will struggle relentlessly to make it stop.

The alcohol jump is one of the scariest because you have no idea if your body has the tendency to become addicted or not. Some may think this one wasn't as big of a deal for them, while others lost their lives and families because the addiction overtook them. I could go on and on about other jumps, such as finances, friendships that you know in your heart are not healthy, cheating in school or work, and stealing. What's crazy is that every jump you take will affect you differently. All of this is to say that if you're staring over the edge, I urge you to take a few steps back and play out the consequences of the jump. If I had done this myself, then I could have avoided so much heartache. I see so many teens these days almost rushing to take jumps they are not ready for. I am sure social media has a lot to do with it because they have so much access to what goes on in other people's lives, but it's okay to slow down! You will be surprised at how much light and wisdom will be shed on your situation simply by taking a few steps back from the edge and asking God to show you how things might play out if you say yes.

Now, there is a flip side to this bridge jumping thing that I can't forget about. When God says jump, YES should be our only response! It's ironic because we tend to jump without thinking when it comes to sin, but when God says jump we need Him to confirm it over and over while we doubt if we truly heard from God. Is anyone else guilty of this or is it just me? It could be as simple as you feeling God put it on your heart to pay for a stranger's meal or serve at your church. It's as if our selfishness starts screaming when God gives us directions and we justify not doing it because we don't want to make someone else uncomfortable or give up the plans we have for ourselves. Choosing obedience when God says to move not only takes an unshakable faith, but it takes a selfless heart willing to be all in regardless of what it means for you. I will be the first one to tell you that it's not easy to jump head-first into obedience, but saying yes to God will absolutely change your life.

I couldn't end this chapter without sharing these last three words that God pressed upon my heart. He kept saying over and over, "be the bridge." Be the bridge in your home when you feel conflict. Instead of inserting yourself and making things worse, shut your mouth and start begging the Holy Spirit to move in your family. Be the bridge at school when you hear gossip amongst friends. Stand up for what is right. Joining in on the gossip will only burn the bridge, but stopping it might help rebuild the bridge. Be the bridge in your workplace, your church, or anywhere that God has you right now. All it takes is one person being the bridge before you start to see healing, movements of God, and hope. Most importantly, be the bridge between others and Jesus. Our decisions have the power to draw people to Jesus or turn them away from Him. This is a huge responsibility as a child of God. Here's the thing: it's nearly impossible to be the bridge in any of these situations if we are not living for the One who bridged the gap between us and our sin. Jesus died for each one of us, and He himself became the bridge for us to spend eternity in Heaven. Without Jesus living in our hearts, we won't have the Holy Spirit guiding and directing us each moment of the day. In order to be the bridge, we need wisdom, guidance, patience, and promptings from the Holy Spirit.

Yes, you are going to jump off some bad bridges just like I have in my life, but allow God to redeem each and every one of them so that the love of God will shine through you. Perfect people don't draw people to Jesus, so don't try to hide your mistakes and failures. Our stories allow God to be exalted and He uses those testimonies to change lives. There is nothing worse than walking into a church where people try to act like they are perfect. Lost people need to see they are no different from you and me. We have all fallen short, end of story. The beauty of God's redemption in my life and in yours is the gift that each lost person needs in their life. It brings tears to my eyes to imagine what my life would look like if no one had been the bridge for me to see Jesus when I needed Him most.

PROCESS AND REFLECT:

- What bridges, or big decisions, are you contemplating right now?
- Name a couple of specific ways you could "be the bridge" in your home starting today? Are there ways you are causing more division than unity?

If you truly want to change, you have to be willing to do whatever it takes regardless of how difficult it is.

21

chapter twenty-one: abandon

"Walk by the Spirit, and you will not carry out the desires of your flesh."

GALATIANS 5:16

As I sit down tonight to begin this penultimate chapter, I am overwhelmed with all the Lord has taught me through this journey. He gave me 21 chapter titles before He even revealed that I was to write a book. He could see the big picture, long before my eyes were ready to see, and He was patient in His timing with me. I have shared many stories and many lessons. There are so many more stories I didn't make space for in this book, but they also played a vital role in my journey. The only chapter title that completely changed directions was this chapter. Somewhere in these final chapters, I began to see the word abandon. Slowly but surely, God revealed the final piece of the puzzle when it comes to living with an audience of one.

When my sister and I were about seven and nine years old, our family took a trip to visit Glenrose, Texas. Glenrose was only about an hour away, but they had a neat wildlife park and swimming areas by the river. I can't remember all the details of that day, but I do remember a traumatic event that would eventually play a role in the way I thought. I can remember swimming in the river with Audra, splashing around and enjoying the day. I remember the fun we had as we rode the waves of the currents from rock to the next rock. We were only in waist-deep water, but due to the currents that day we started drifting downstream without realizing it. Once we looked up and saw how far we were from the others, we tried making our way back to more shallow waters. It was too late. Neither Audra nor myself were strong enough to pull the other one back to where we needed to be. The currents picked up and we started moving faster. That's when the panic sunk in. If I close my eyes, I can still see Audra's face looking to me for help. I wasn't capable of helping either one of us. I knew it was serious and we only had minutes before I was going to be too weak to hold onto her.

We could see our dad running on the rocks above trying to get to us. Only as he ran, he got higher and higher. I knew there was no way he would be able to jump safely into the water to come for us. Helpless is the only word I can use to describe how I felt as I was clinging to a rock under the water with my legs. Audra was clinging to me, but the current was pulling us both under. I knew if I let go, I would lose her. I knew we needed to be rescued. Choking on water and barely able to catch my breath, I remember looking towards the shallow waters and seeing two men coming for us. I have no idea where they came from, but as I saw them getting closer I knew they were going to do everything they could to save us. I guess you already know the ending since I am still here today, but that was the day I knew what it was like to be physically rescued. It would be another few decades before I knew what it was like to be spiritually rescued.

I am sure you can imagine how that trauma has shaped us. To this day, neither of us can relax if our kids are playing in darker waters and the fear of rivers and currents is usually a trigger for me. It's something people have made fun of when I have freaked out in those moments, but going through something like that changes you. You don't see a river like everyone else sees a river anymore and there's nothing you can do to really change that. Remember the blurry lens? The trauma from this situation is another way my lens was affected long term.

When I sat down to write these final words tonight, there was no doubt in my mind what story God would have me use to help put into words this final piece of the puzzle. The sole purpose of this book is to teach us how to have an audience of one in every part of our lives. We have talked about so many different ways we can pursue that mindset, but unless we abandon our flesh daily we will find ourselves seeking the wrong audience time and time again. To abandon means to flee from. Abandon means to waive our rights and fully surrender.

My friend, Beth, once told me that I had strong flesh patterns, which meant my flesh would scream louder than logic and convictions, and that my emotions would be too involved in my decision making. I could have easily been offended by this, but I knew it was true. Her words sunk in and I reflected on the implication of what she said, I had to decide what I was going to do. It would have been easier to say that's just how I am, but I knew those strong flesh patterns were unhealthy and needed to be dealt with. One by one, I started doing the hard work, putting boundaries in place, and fighting my flesh with worship and prayer.

Maybe you're reading this and you're unsure what fleshly behaviors are, so let me explain before going on. The list is endless, but a few examples would be being quick to anger, taking things personally when it's not about you, an addictive nature to different types of sin, jealousy, selfishness, or even a potty mouth. Any time our flesh is fighting what is right for us, you can think of that as fleshly patterns in our lives. Fleshly patterns look differently in each of us, which is why we all have different struggles or addictions.

Any time our flesh is fighting what is right for us, you can think of that as fleshly patterns in our lives.

I don't know if you realize it or not, but our flesh can be powerful and can cling to sin very quickly in ways we never imagined. If you don't believe me, open Instagram and scroll for 10 minutes. I would be shocked if you can go 10 straight minutes without your flesh entering your mind or thoughts. This means you can't compare, you can't get jealous, you can't be mad because someone is on a trip and you're not, you can't get annoyed with the girl who has the so-called perfect life, and you can't judge the girl who is half dressed and begging for attention in the wrong places. I think I covered most things that cycle through the minds of females as they scroll. How do I know this? One, I am female. Two, I have heard these struggles from women for years. I once asked Brylee and her friends to describe social media in one word and Brylee said "exhausting!" She was so right! Even if you are fighting your flesh and thinking nice thoughts, it's still hard work! Social media is only one way our flesh can overtake us, but I think you get the point.

I cannot have an audience of one if I am walking in the flesh.

God continues to show me that I must abandon my flesh every day, from when I get up till I go to bed. When I do, He reveals a new understanding of how to seek an audience of one. I cannot have an audience of one if I am walking in the flesh. I can't go a minute in my flesh or else my mind will succumb to fear, anxiety, people pleasing, insecurity, or some sort of emotion that I know is not from the Lord. This is exactly why the Bible says to walk in the Spirit so that we don't gratify the desires of our flesh! God knew; He has always known! Scripture is clear when it says to flee from sin and chase after the heart of Jesus! When Eve took a bite of the apple from the tree and chose darkness things were never the same. Every time I have fallen and given in to my flesh, things were never the same for me. This is the consequence of sin.

Every time I have fallen and given in to my flesh, things were never the same for me.

If you are anything like me and have strong fleshly patterns, then you must decide who is going to be in charge of you! Are you going to let your flesh make the calls and decisions throughout your day, or will you choose to walk in the Spirit in order to live in purity? I wish I could say that I have been walking in the Spirit for a really long time, but that is not the case. Up until I was about 36 years old, it was my flesh that governed my mind, my reactions, my decisions, and my emotions. Over the last eight years, I have taken baby steps in an effort to see strong Spirit patterns shine through me instead of my yucky flesh. Learning to do this has taken time and humility, but God has honored my effort.

Our world operates completely against this mindset of living with an audience of one. I know how hard it is to retrain the mind. I couldn't have written each of these chapters when they happened because it has taken years for God to penetrate my soul as He taught me each lesson the hard way. I know it seems impossible to not seek the approval of others. Our flesh wants to be liked, wants to be accepted, and wants the approval of others. This is how this book started, so I get it, but I have also lived out those fleshly desires and they landed me on the floor of a closet hoping that I wouldn't have to live one more day in this world. It's a dangerous place to be when our audience is anything or anyone but Jesus. I pray to God that you have seen my heart throughout this book so that you can minimize your pain and learn from someone who has already done it the wrong way.

I want to leave you with one last thought. When I was laying on that closet floor feeling completely broken, it wasn't the world who came to my rescue. I had spent years living with the fear of man, trying to please everyone around me, but that night on that floor there was only one person who saw me. His name was Jesus. He was my rescuer, He redeemed my soul, and He gave me a second chance. His eyes and His audience is the only audience worth living and fighting for.

PROCESS AND REFLECT:

- Do you feel you have strong flesh patterns that continue to get in your way of living a pure life? If so, write a few of them down and ask yourself how much your flesh is shining through over the course of your day.

bonus chapter

bonus chapter raising girls

"Fix your thoughts on what is true, and honorable, and right, and pure, and lovely, and admirable. Think about things that are excellent and praiseworthy."

PHILIPPIANS 4:18

As I sit here typing this, my girls are 11, 13, and 15. I am only a few years into the world of "raising teen girls", so please know that I have a long way to go. With that said, I learned so much when my eldest, Brylee, was in the 7th grade. Since then, the lessons have continued to come. I would like to share 10 pieces of advice from what I have learned thus far. Take it or leave it, but I would have loved for someone to tell me these things before we hit the teen years!

1. YOU WILL GET THROUGH IT, AND YES, THERE IS LIGHT ON THE OTHER SIDE

I used to be a 7th-grade teacher. I can remember how hard it was to teach science to a room of precious children with raging emotional hormones! There were days when the science lesson didn't matter because they needed hugs, conflict resolution with friends, and life advice. Seventh grade can be a tough year. If it's your first time with a middle schooler, you might feel like it's never going to get better, but it does. Emotions settle, girls mature, and friendships grow. Before you know it, the 7th-grade turmoil is just a memory. I took it so seriously with Brylee, but it has been so much easier with Cerly. There is something about knowing that this, too, shall pass that keeps me from worrying too much the second time around.

2. TALK HONESTLY AND OPENLY TO YOUR DAUGHTER STARTING FROM AN EARLY AGE

It's important to consider age-appropriate conversations, but starting with small talk will open the door of communication early. I've noticed that opening the door early makes it much easier for both mom and daughter to discuss sensitive topics. My girls have so many questions, just like most kidsd, and I want them to hear the answers from me, not the internet or friends at school. The only way they will feel comfortable coming to us is if we set the stage and create a safe place to do so. We can't confront them with challenging topics during their teen years and expect them to respond comfortably if we haven't provided a healthy runway leading up to those important conversations.

3. OUR DAUGHTERS ARE UNIQUE AND DIFFERENT

This is especially important for those with multiple girls in the home. Because they are different, they have different needs and ways of handling things. Be prepared to adjust as you navigate each relationship differently, considering the time of day they feel best opening up, how to settle them down when they're upset, and the type of affection they need. When we try to treat them the same, it can cause frustration, conflict, and even withdrawal. I used to try and make all of them like me, but that never went well for anyone. Brylee and Audree need lots of affection, but I have to think before I go in with too much affection when it comes to Cerly. What is comfortable to Audree and Brylee will be too much for Cerly. They all respond differently to spiritual things, and their emotional reactions are night and day. Get to know your daughter so that you can meet her in a place where everyone feels comfortable.

4. BE CAREFUL NOT TO REACT TO HEATED SITUATIONS UNTIL YOU HAVE ALL THE PIECES TO THE PUZZLE OR AS MANY AS YOU ARE ABLE TO GET

I have accused my kids of things before getting the whole story, simply because another kid said it was true. I learned the hard way that all kids are capable of lying, and it is crucial not to react until you have a better understanding of the situation. Taking some time to think before responding will allow us moms to be fair in our approach, and everyone involved will be more respectful of how we handled it. When we instantly react, we often create additional conflict that will also have to be resolved.

5. WE HAVE TO REMEMBER THAT THE WORLD OUR GIRLS ARE GROWING UP IN LOOKS MUCH DIFFERENT THAN THE ONE WE GREW UP IN

This changes so many things. We can't get stuck in our ways or the ways we said we would parent without considering the changes happening around us. The world around them is drastically different from what it was when we were their ages. Phones, social media, school shootings, and the repercussions of COVID are just a few things that we never had to face growing up. When I think back to being a high school girl, I cannot imagine trying to navigate those years with the devices and the environment our kids are growing up in. We must be patient, we must be willing to shift our parenting at times, and we have to listen so that we can understand things that might be foreign to us.

6. IT DOESN'T MATTER HOW GOOD A KID YOU HAVE; THEY ARE NOT PERFECT

Every child is capable of making both good and poor choices. The sooner we moms accept this, the better. When we embrace this, we're less likely to get defensive when another mom comes to us about our child. I have witnessed amazing children lie, cheat, change stories for attention, and completely make things up out of spite. The toughest thing is when you have to approach a mom who thinks her kid can do no wrong. Before you quickly defend your kid, take some time to talk to them. It is important to fight for them when we need to, but it's also important that we fully understand that our children have a sinful nature just like we do. The last thing we want is to come across as prideful and unapproachable when our goal should be to help our child be their very best. Part of becoming the best versions of ourselves means hearing hard things, taking responsibility, and changing our behavior.

7. THE APPLE DOESN'T FALL FAR FROM THE TREE, WHETHER IT IS GOOD OR BAD!

If we are anxious, they will feed off of us, and their world will become chaotic. If they hear us talking disrespectfully about others, I promise you the will hear unkind things come out of their mouths as well. On the flip side, when they see us asking for forgiveness then they too will learn what it looks like to reconcile with humility. They are watching every move and listening to every word. Let's humble ourselves for their sake and allow their eyes to become extra accountability in our lives.

8. BE HONEST WITH YOUR KIDS AND AVOID CREATING UNNECESSARY WALLS BECAUSE OF SECRETS

I could use many examples here, but I will go with the first one that came to my mind. The older I get, the more I have seen my physical body fall apart. Topics like boob jobs, fillers, and Botox seem to be coming up more than ever. I have decided that I will never lie to the girls because lying builds walls and causes division. If they ask, I will be honest. Yes, I agree that age matters, but there will come a time when they are closer to eighteen than eight. Being honest with them is important to me. Not everyone will agree with this, but I've noticed that people find it easier to handle the truth than a lie. Parenting doesn't end when they go to college, and I want them to trust me indefinitely.

9. "DON'T JUMP ON THE EMOTIONAL TRAIN WITH THEM."

This is some of the best advice I've ever been given. When Brylee came home crying during 7th grade, I often found myself feeling it all with her and crying too. I didn't step back and listen. I jumped into her situation, which ultimately led to jumping right into the emotions of it as well. Brandon never knew what to do with either of us during these moments, and it wasn't helpful to Brylee for me to be so emotionally involved. A sweet friend in my Sunday school class told me that I needed to stay off of the train! She said things will spiral out of control when I jump on the train with her. This one piece of advice changed our lives and the emotional health of our home. I have seen that staying out of the emotion allows me to think logically, have a clear mind, and guide her in a more wise direction.

10. WE SHOULD BE THE CALMEST ONE IN THE HOME

I know, I know, this can be difficult, but the stability of the home often rests on the stability of the mom. When I am calm and slow to speak, it is like everyone follows suit. When I am reactive and dramatic, the whole home falls apart. When I think of this, I think of Follow the Leader. It's such a silly little game, but this is how many homes operate. Every single day, Brandon and I are fully aware that our home is more successful when we are healthy and on the same page. Moms, pray constantly, be in the Word, and do the hard work so that your security is in Him. A healthy home starts with a healthy mom!

That's all I have for now! I pray that when I am on the other side of raising these sweet girls I will be able to share more of the many lessons I learned. I love when moms can grow by coming together along the way and helping each other see new ways of doing things. I hope one of these tips allows your home to be one step closer to where you desire it to be. Always remember, taking one baby step at a time will get you where you want to be if you seek Him in every step. Continue moving forward for yourself and your children because what you do matters!

ABOUT THE AUTHOR

Tanna Horton

Tanna Horton grew up in the Dallas area with a loving family, and has been involved with church her entire life. She married her best friend, Brandon, who she first met in her church youth group in the 7th grade. Together they have four children: Brylee, Cerly, Audree, and Heath. Her children attend a university model school, which allows her to partially homeschool them during the week, and focus on them as her main ministry. She also enjoys traveling, exercising and spending time in laughter with the people she loves. Tanna has always had a passion for teaching, and over the last 15 years has developed a heart for women in a unique way. She loves sharing the life lessons that God has taught her with other women to help them grow spiritually as a wife, mom, and friend.

www.ingramcontent.com/pod-product-compliance
Ingram Content Group UK Ltd.
Pitfield, Milton Keynes, MK11 3LW, UK
UKHW051206260726
13967UKWH00011B/3126